Praise for Michael E. Gerber, Riley F. Uglum, and *The E-Myth Optometrist*

If your world is filled with stress caused by your practice, then this book
is a must read. **The key is strategic planning.** This book gives you the
background needed to effectively enact practice changing and therefore,
life changing, strategic planning. Stop allowing stress to damage your life
and start living smarter by applying the principles taught in this book.

Mark R. Wright, OD, FCOVD, clinical associate professor,
College of Optometry at The Ohio State University

It's uncommon to find a visionary who can see so far down the road in
his industry, and yet also has walked that path. Riley Uglum is one such
entrepreneur. **Read *The E-Myth Optometrist* and get a five-year head
start out of the chaos, scarcity and fear and toward financial and personal
freedom.**

Jon LoDuca, CEO of The Wisdom Link, author and innovation expert

Riley has had an exemplary and progressive optometry practice throughout
the 25+ years I have known him. His unique insight has proven to be highly
valuable when considering new instrumentation and services to bring to
our customers. He leverages a well-trained staff and the latest technologies
to provide a patient care experience that gives him a competitive
advantage in the marketplace. **The optometric practice strategies taught
in *The E-Myth Optometrist* enable optometrists to feel confident about
facing the challenges of today's health care environment.**

Jon Dymit, VP and general manager for the Walman Instrument Group

The E-Myth Optometrist and Promethean Ventures is helping me get my professional and personal life together. **I'm finally able to see a way out of all of the school debt and practice start up costs I've incurred.** It's amazing to discover these business strategies which seem new to me now, but have been used by successful business owners for a long time.

Travis Johnson, OD

As a young practitioner with a new office, *The E-Myth Optometrist* has guided my growing business for the best possible future success! This book offers great benefits for any OD in private practice.

Gina Wesley, OD

I have personally used the strategies described in *The E-Myth Optometrist* and can attest to their effectiveness. Promethean Ventures concepts have helped put my practice on steroids financially. **I'm finally able to start thinking about working on my business instead of in it. And I'm focusing on what life will be like when I'm no longer a slave to my practice.**

James W. Vann, OD

I've been a Promethean Ventures client for the past two years and have learned a lot about what my practice needs to improve financially. ***The E-Myth Optometrist* just adds to this knowledge base and is helping me systemize all of the things that will help me grow my business in the future.**

Jim Kivlin, OD

Michael Gerber's *E-Myth* is one of only four books I recommend as required reading. **For those looking to start and build a business of their own, this is the man who has coached more successful entrepreneurs than the next ten gurus combined.**

Timothy Ferris, #1 *New York Times* best-selling author of *The 4-Hour Workweek*

One of the first concepts that I learned in my MBA curriculum was the purpose of studying business administration. That purpose is simply, to reduce uncertainty. ***The E-Myth Optometrist* delivers the means to envision, plan, implement and control a strategy which will radically improve the probability for success in your practice with the challenges that the future may present.**

Jerome A. Legerton, OD, MS, MBA, FAAO

Everyone needs a mentor, someone who tells it like it is, holds you accountable, and shows you your good, bad and ugly. For millions of small business owners Michael Gerber is that person. Let Michael be your mentor and you are in for a kick in the pants, the ride of a lifetime.

John Jantsch, author of *Duct Tape Marketing*

Michael Gerber is a master instructor and a leader's leader. As a combat F15 fighter pilot, I had to navigate complex missions with life-and-death consequences, but until I read *The E-Myth* and met Michael Gerber, my transition to the world of small business was a nightmare with no real flight plan. The hands-on, practical magic of Michael's turnkey systems magnified by the raw power of his keen insight and wisdom have changed my life forever.

Steve Olds, CEO, Stratworx.com

Michael Gerber's strategies in *The E-Myth* were instrumental in building my company from two employees to a global organization; I can't wait to see how applying the strategies from *Awakening the Entrepreneur Within* will affect its growth!

Dr. Ivan Misner, founder and chairman of BNI, and author of *Masters of Sales*

Michael Gerber's gift to isolate the issues and present simple, direct, business changing solutions shines bright with *Awakening the Entrepreneur Within*. If you're interested in developing an entrepreneurial vision and plan that inspires others to action, buy this book, read it, and apply the processes Gerber brilliantly defines.

Tim Templeton, author of *The Referral of a Lifetime*

Michael Gerber truly, truly understands what it takes to be a successful practicing entrepreneur and business owner. He has demonstrated to me over six years of working with him that for those who stay the course and learn much more than just "how to work on their business and not in it" then they will reap rich rewards. I finally franchised my business and the key to unlocking this kind of potential in any business is the teachings of Michael's work.

Chris Owen, marketing director, Royal Armouries (International) plc

My wife, Colleen, and I spent twenty-five years flying in the United States Air Force and with commercial airlines. When we changed our career focus and decided to open our own business, we read dozens of books and attended countless seminars. Nothing came close to the quality and precision of the environment that we had lived in for all those years – until we read Michael Gerber's books. His insightful writings finally gave us the flight plan that we had been missing. **We carry copies of his books in our car and share them with other entrepreneurs, because we know that their lives and businesses can be changed in a profound way by the wisdom of Michael Gerber.**

Bill and Colleen Hensley, founders of Hensley Properties, Inc.,
authors of *The Pilot-Learning Leadership*

Michael's work has been an inspiration to us. **His books have helped us get free from the out-of-control life that we once had. His no-nonsense approach kept us focused on our ultimate aim rather than day-to-day stresses. He has helped take our business to levels we couldn't have imagined possible.** In the Dreaming Room made us totally reevaluate how we thought about our business and our life. We have now redesigned our life se we can manifest the dreams we unearthed in Michael's Dreaming Room.

Jo and Steve Davison, founders of The Spinal Health Clinic
Chiropractic Group and www.your-dream-life.com

Rarely—maybe once in a lifetime— is there a message that transforms us, that inspires us to create the vision that describes the grandest version of ourselves, and then act upon it. Several years ago, we heard such a message, Michael Gerber's message. Since then, our journey with Michael has truly awakened the entrepreneur within us! We can't wait to take our lives and the lives of our clients to the next level through this book!

Robert and Susan Clements, principals, E-Myth Iowa

Because of Michael Gerber, I transformed my twenty-four-hour-a-day, seven-day-a-week job (also called a small business) into a multimillion turnkey business. This in turn set the foundation for my worldwide training firm. **I am living my dream because of Michael Gerber.**

Howard Partridge, Phenomenal Products, Inc.

Michael Gerber is an outrageous revolutionary who is changing the way the world does business. **He dares you to commit to your grandest dreams and then shows you how to make the impossible a reality. If you let him, this man will change your life.**

Fiona Fallon, founder of Divine and The Bottom Line

Michael Gerber is a genius. Every successful business person I meet has read Michael Gerber, refers to Michael Gerber and lives by his words. You just can't get enough of Michael Gerber. **He has the innate (and rare) ability to tap into one's soul, look deeply and tell you what you need to hear. And then, he inspires you, equips you with the tools to get it done.**

Pauline O'Malley, CEO, TheRevenueBuilder

When asked "Who was the most influential person in your life?" I am one of the thousands who don't hesitate to say "Michael E. Gerber." **Michael helped transform me from someone dreaming of retirement to someone dreaming of working until age one hundred.** This awakening is the predictable outcome of anyone reading Michael's new book.

Thomas O. Bardeen

Michael Gerber is an incredible business philosopher, guru, perhaps even a seer. He has an amazing intuition which allows him to see in an instant what everybody else is missing; he sees opportunity everywhere. **While in The Dreaming Room, Michael gave me the gift of seeing through the eyes of an awakened entrepreneur, and instantly my business changed from a regional success to serving clients on four continents.**

Keith G. Schiehl, president, Rent-a-Geek Computer Services

Michael Gerber is among the very few who truly understand entrepreneurship and small business. While others talk about these topics in the form of theories, methodologies, processes, and so on, Michael goes to the heart of the issues. **Whenever Michael writes about entrepreneurship, soak it in as it is not only good for your business, but great for your soul.** His words will help you to keep your passion and balance while sailing through the uncertain sea of entrepreneurship.

Raymond Yeh, co-author, *The Art of Business*

Michael Gerber's insight, wisdom, caring and straightforward approach helped me reinvent myself and my business while doubling my revenues in less than one year. Crack open this book and let him do the same for you, too.

Christine Kloser, author *The Freedom Formula and Conscious Entrepreneurs*

Michael Gerber forced me to think big, think real, and gave me the support network to make it happen. A new wave of entrepreneurs is rising, much in thanks to his amazing efforts and very practical approach to doing business.

Christian Kessner, Higher Ground Retreats and Events

Michael's understanding of entrepreneurship and small business management has been a difference maker for countless businesses, including Infusion Software. His insights into the entrepreneurial process of building a business are a must read for every small business owner. The vision, clarity, and leadership that came out of our Dreaming Room experience were just what our company needed to recognize our potential and motivate the whole company to achieve it.

Clate Mask, president and CEO, Infusion Software

Michael Gerber is a truly remarkable man. His steady openness of mind and ability to get to the deeper level continues to be an inspiration and encouragement to me. He seems to always ask that one question that forces the new perspective to break open and he approaches the new coming method in a fearless way.

Rabbi Levi Cunin, Chabad of Malibu

The Dreaming Room experience was literally life changing for us. Within months, we were able to start our Foundation and make several television appearances owing to his teachings. He has an incredible charisma which is priceless, but above all Michael Gerber *awakens* passion from within enabling you to take action with dramatic results… starting today!

Shona and Shaun Carcary, Trinity Property Investments Inc.
– Home Vestors franchises

I thought *E-Myth* was an awkward name! What could this book do for me? **But when I finally got to reading it... it was what I was looking for all along.** Then, to top it off, I took a twenty-seven-hour trip to San Diego just to attend the Dreaming Room, where Michael touched my heart, my mind, and my soul.

Helmi Natto, president, Eye 2 Eye Optics, Saudi Arabia

I attended In the Dreaming Room and was challenged by Michael Gerber to "Go out and do what's impossible." So I did; **I became an author and international speaker and used Michael's principles to create a world-class company that will change and save lives all over the world.**

Dr. Don Kennedy, MBA, author, *5AM & Already Behind,* www.bahbits.com

I went to the Dreaming Room to have Michael Gerber fix my business. He talked about dreaming. What was this dreaming? I was too busy working! Too busy being miserable, angry, frustrated, behind in what I was trying to accomplish. And losing everything I was working for. **Then Michael Gerber woke up the dreamer in me and remade my life and my business.**

Pat Doorn, president, Mountain View Electric, Ltd.

Michael Gerber can captivate a room full of entrepreneurs and take them to a place where they can focus on the essentials that are the underpinning of every successful business. He gently leads them from where they are to where they need to be in order to change the world.

Francine Hardaway, CEO, Stealthmode Partners and founder of the Arizona Entrepreneurship Conferences

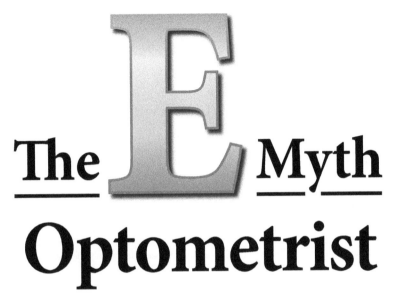

The **E** Myth
Optometrist

*Why Most Optometry
Practices Don't Work
and What to Do About It*

MICHAEL E. GERBER

RILEY F. UGLUM, OD

PRODIGY
BUSINESS BOOKS

Published by
Prodigy Business Books, Inc., Carlsbad, California.

Production Team
Trish Beaulieu, book division manager, Dezign Matters Creative Group, Inc.;
Helen Chang, editor, helenchangwriter.com; Erich Broesel, cover designer,
BroselDesign, Inc.; Nancy Ratkiewich, book production, njr productions;
Jeff Kassebaum, Michael E. Gerber author photographer, Jeff Kassebaum and Co.;
Christy Roethler, Riley Uglum co-author photographer, Images by Christy

For general information on other products and services, please visit the website:
www.michaelegerber.com.

ISBN 978-0-9835001-0-0 (pbk)
ISBN 978-0-9835001-1-7 (cloth)
ISBN 978-0-9835542-0-2 (ebk)

Printed in the United States of America

10 9 8 7 6 5 4 3 2 1

To Luz Delia, whose heart expands mine,
whose soul inspires mine,
whose boldness reaches for the stars, thank you,
forever, for being, truly mine…

—Michael E. Gerber

CONTENTS

A WORD ABOUT THIS BOOK

Michael E. Gerber

My first E-Myth book was published in 1985. It was called *The E-Myth: Why Most Small Businesses Don't Work and What to Do About It*. Since that book, and the company I created to provide business development services to its many readers, millions have read *The E-Myth*, and the book that followed it called *The E-Myth Revisited*, and tens of thousands have participated in our E-Myth Mastery programs.

The co-author of this book, *The E-Myth Optometrist*, Riley F. Uglum, OD, is one of my more enthusiastic readers, and as a direct result of his enthusiasm, his optometry practice became one of those clients. He became, over the years, one of my friends.

This book is two things: the product of my lifelong work conceiving, developing, and growing the E-Myth way into a business model that has been applied to every imaginable kind of company in the world, as well as a product of Riley's extraordinary experience and success applying the E-Myth to development of his equally extraordinary enterprise, Eye Care Associates of New Hampton.

So it was that one day, while sitting with my muse, which I think of as my inner voice, and which many who know me think of as "here he goes again!" that I thought about the creation of an entire series of E-Myth expert books. That series, including this book, would be co-authored by experts in every industry who had successfully applied my E-Myth principles to the extreme development of a practice—a very small company—with the intent of growing it nationwide, and even worldwide, which is what Riley had in mind as he began to discover the almost infinite range of opportunities provided by thinking the E-Myth way.

Upon seeing the possibilities of this new idea, I immediately invited co-authors such as Riley to join me. He said, "Let's do it!" and so we did.

Welcome to *The E-Myth Optometrist: Why Most Optometry Practices Don't Work and What to Do About It.*

Read it, enjoy it, and let us—Riley and I—help you apply the E-Myth to the re-creation, development, and extreme growth of your optometric practice into an enterprise that you can be justifiably proud of.

To your life, your wisdom, and the life and success of your clients, I wish you good reading.

—Michael E. Gerber
Co-Founder/Chairman
Michael E. Gerber Companies, Inc.
Carlsbad, California
www.michaelegerber.com/co-author

A NOTE FROM RILEY

It all began at an optometry mastermind meeting in 2005. I was in Chicago sitting around a large conference room table with eight of my peers discussing growth strategies for our practices. We all considered ourselves to be entrepreneurs. After all, we were good doctors and had practices that performed better than most. And we were learning how to improve our performance even more by exchanging ideas in a facilitated environment.

But at this point in my career, I was just going through the motions. I'd grown my practice to a level that was double the national average while seeing patients just three days a week. But those three days were very stressful down in the trenches, and I had trouble getting out of bed on the days I knew I would be seeing patients. Plus, there were all the other headaches involved with running an optometry business, like staff management, insurance plans, accounts receivable, accounts payable, and on and on and on.

I was also suffering from an affliction known as "The Arrival Syndrome." I had arrived at OD (doctor of optometry), the highest level attainable for a solo practice (or so I thought), and there wasn't much more I could learn or that anyone could teach me. Sure, I might be able to tweak things here and there to further improve my practice's performance, but I was basically looking at grinding it out a few more years in a profession that was burning me out.

So as I sat in Chicago at this meeting, our facilitator began talking about how systems could make us better and referred to a book called *The E-Myth Revisited* by Michael E. Gerber. I remember thinking that it was an odd name for a book, but when I saw it in an airport bookstore on my return home, I bought it. Once I started reading, I couldn't stop. This Gerber guy had a crazy notion about operating a business that I could not really believe was true. I could see how his business model worked for companies like McDonald's and Federal Express. But a health care business like optometry was different. How could he possibly compare safeguarding the vision of my patients with making a Big Mac?

But one nagging thought kept occurring to me. *What if he were right?* If this story he was telling in the book were really true, *I wanted a piece of that action!*

And as it turned out, of course, the story was true. After enrolling in the E-Myth Mastery coaching program, my practice grew 50 percent while continuing to see patients three days a week. I was definitely working smarter and not harder. But the most important part of this whole experience was that I was having fun again with my chosen profession. I had more staff and some solid business tools at my disposal to deal with my key frustrations. I was bringing another doctor into the practice so I could spend more time "working on the business" instead of "working in the business." E-Myth Mastery also helped me discover my "primary aim" in life and taught me that my business needs to support that aim. I came to realize that growing and innovating a business, which deeply touches its patients, its staff, and its owners, is what makes life more meaningful for all of those people. How cool is that?

It was also at this time that my wife Kathy and I discovered and employed a financial concept called prosperity economics that was very synergistic with E-Myth philosophy. When combined with our entity structuring that was already in place, we were able to put E-Myth on steroids by providing additional capital to fuel our business and personal growth. This then allowed us to transform the practice into a business—which meant it was no longer solely dependent on my technical doctor skills to survive.

As good as this ride was, it proceeded to get better. I decided to attend one of Michael's Dreaming Rooms in Flagstaff, Arizona, and got to interact with him personally. This led to a mentoring relationship and ultimately to this book. The Dreaming Room was what really allowed me to think on a much grander scale than I ever thought possible. It gave me permission to play with ideas that would have been previously dismissed out of hand. And it put me in touch with others who were going through their own awakening process and dealing with the fears that arise during a major paradigm shift. The Dreaming Room truly awakened "The Entrepreneur Within" and makes me wonder how I ever lived life without him.

A new company, Promethean Ventures, was born from that Dreaming Room experience and it represents the transformation of an optometry business into an enterprise. Its mission is to share with other optometrists the systemized business concepts that will transform their practice into:

- A business that is independent of *their* optometry skills
- A business that provides them with the entrepreneurial skills to set them free
- A business that optometry schools or traditional practice management firms don't teach us how to build

This is not to say that your practice doesn't need the skills taught in optometry schools or practice management firms. It does. Good clinical and business building skills are critical to your practice. Just think of Promethean Ventures as the entrepreneurial MBA graduate school for optometry that will provide you with the *freedom* to pursue your true purpose in life. Another way to think of it is that Promethean concepts allow you to practice optometry as a hobby and to define yourself as an entrepreneur—instead of as an optometrist.

Please keep an open mind as you read this book. The temptation will be to put it down and say "I could never do that." I know because I used to say the same thing when I practiced in a 1,200-square-foot facility with two staff members. The concepts presented here are real, and they work. I'm no more special than any of you are. Believe me, I have lived with the same fears and concerns that you may be experiencing right now. And if I can do this, so can you. And you will be so very glad that you did. Life will never be the same for you again (in a good way)!

Our profession is a noble and meaningful one, and I'm committed to protect its viability for future ODs. I believe that the only way to do this is to grow our practices into entrepreneurial businesses that provide superior value for us, our associate ODs, our staff, and our patients. This book will enable you to do just that.

—Riley F. Uglum, OD
Founder
Eye Care Associates of New Hampton
New Hampton, Iowa

PREFACE

Michael E. Gerber

I am not an optometrist, though I have helped dozens of optometrists reinvent their optometry practices over the past thirty-five years.

I like to think of myself as a thinker, maybe even a dreamer. Yes, I like to *do* things. But before I jump in and get my hands dirty, I prefer to think through what I'm going to do and figure out the best way to do it. I imagine the impossible, dream big, and then try to figure out how the impossible can become the possible. After that, it's about how to turn the possible into reality.

Over the years, I've made it my business to study how things work and how people work—specifically, how things and people work best together to produce optimum results. That means creating an organization that can do great things and achieve more than any other organization can.

This book is about how to produce the best results as a real-world optometrist in the development, expansion, and liberation of your practice. In the process, you will come to understand what the practice of optometry—as a *business*—is and what it isn't. If you keep focusing on what it isn't, you're destined for failure. But if you turn your sights on what it *is*, the tide will turn.

This book, intentionally small, is about big ideas. The topics we'll be discussing in this book are the very issues that optometrists face daily in their practice. You know what they are: money, management, patients, and many more. My aim is to help you begin the exciting process of totally transforming the way you do business. As such, I'm confident that *The E-Myth Optometrist* could well be the most important book on the practice of optometry as a business that you'll ever read.

Unlike other books on the market, my goal is not to tell you how to do the work you do. Instead, I want to share with you the E-Myth philosophy as a way to revolutionize the way you think about the work you do. I'm convinced that this new way of thinking is something optometrists everywhere must adopt in order for their optometry practice to flourish during these trying times. I call it strategic thinking, as opposed to tactical thinking.

In strategic thinking, also called systems thinking, you, the optometrist, will begin to think about your entire practice— the broad scope of it—instead of focusing on its individual parts. You will begin to see the end game (perhaps for the first time) rather than just the day-to-day routine that's consuming you—the endless, draining work I call "doing it, doing it, doing it."

Understanding strategic thinking will enable you to create a practice that becomes a successful business, with the potential to flourish as an even more successful enterprise. But in order for you to accomplish this, your practice, your business, and certainly your enterprise must work *apart* from you instead of *because* of you.

The E-Myth philosophy says that a highly successful optometry practice can grow into a highly successful optometry business, which in turn can become the foundation for an inordinately successful optometry enterprise that runs smoothly and efficiently *without* the optometrist having to be in the office for ten hours a day, six days a week.

So what is "The E-Myth" exactly? The E-Myth is short for the Entrepreneurial Myth, which says that most businesses fail to fulfill their potential because most people starting their own business are not entrepreneurs at all. They're actually what I call *technicians suffering from an entrepreneurial seizure*. When technicians suffering from an entrepreneurial seizure start an optometry practice of their own, they almost always end up working themselves into a frenzy;

their days are booked solid with appointments, one patient after another. These optometrists are burning the candle at both ends, fueled by too much coffee and too little sleep, and most of the time, they can't even stop to think.

In short, The E-Myth says that most optometrists don't own a true business—most own a job. They're doing it, doing it, doing it, hoping like hell to get some time off, but never figuring out how to get their business to run without them. And if your business doesn't run well without you, what happens when you can't be in two places at once? Ultimately, your practice will fail.

There are a number of prestigious schools throughout the nation dedicated to teaching the science of optometry. The problem is, they fail to teach the *business* of it. And because they are not being taught how to run their practice as a business, many optometrists find themselves having to close their doors every year. You could be a world-class expert in pediatric eye care or glaucoma, but when it comes to building a successful business, all that specified knowledge matters exactly zilch.

The good news is that you don't have to be among the statistics of failure in the optometric profession. The E-Myth philosophy I am about to share with you in this book has been successfully applied to many optometry practices just like yours with extraordinary results.

The key to transforming your practice—and your life—is to grasp the profound difference between going to work *on* your practice (systems thinker) and going to work *in* your practice (tactical thinker). In other words, it's the difference between going to work on your practice as an entrepreneur and going to work in your practice as an optometrist.

The two are not mutually exclusive. In fact, they are essential to each other. The problem with most optometry practices is that the systems thinker—the entrepreneur—is completely absent. And so is the vision.

The E-Myth philosophy says that the key to transforming your practice into a successful enterprise is knowing how to transform yourself from successful optometric technician into a successful technician-manager-entrepreneur. In the process, everything you do in your optometry practice will be transformed. The door is then open to turning it into the kind of practice it should be—a practice, a business, an enterprise of pure joy!

The E-Myth not only *can* work for you; it *will* work for you. In the process, it will give you an entirely new experience of your business and beyond. So put on your eyeglasses: it's time to look sharp.

To your future and your life! Good reading.

—Michael E. Gerber
Co-Founder/Chairman
Michael E. Gerber Companies, Inc.
Carlsbad, California
www.michaelegerber.com/co-author

ACKNOWLEDGMENTS

Michael E. Gerber

As always, and never to be forgotten, there are those who give of themselves to make my work possible.

To my dearest and most forgiving partner, wife, friend and co-founder, Luz Delia Gerber, whose love and commitment takes me to places I would often not go unaccompanied.

To Jim Taylor, whose persistency and at times demonic steady state of heart, made the impossible less improbable, and the possible, if not easy, more predictable than we hoped. To James Taylor, whose light was often lit, whose hope was not too easily dismissed, and who stayed the course, of course, because that is his way.

To Helen Chang, noble warrior, editor, brave soul and sojourner, who covers all the bases we would have missed had she not been there. To Erich Broesel, our stand-alone graphic designer and otherwise visual genius who supported the creation of all things visual that will forever be all things Gerber, we thank you, deeply, for your continuous contribution of things both temporal and eternal. To Trish Beaulieu, wow, you are splendid. And to Nancy Ratkiewich, whose work has been essential for you who are reading this.

To Johanna Nilsson who told us that social media was much, much more than just social, and then, with the grace G-d gave her, proved it every step of the way. To Kimberly Butler, who organizes, administers, and just chuckles about it all, we thank you from the bottom of our often disorganized appearance and always joyous hearts.

To those many, many dreamers, thinkers, storytellers and leaders, whose travels with me in The Dreaming Room have given me life, breath and pleasure unanticipated before we met. To those many participants in my life (you know who you are), thank you for taking me seriously, and joining me in this exhilarating quest.

And, of course, to my co-authors, all of you, your genius, wisdom, intelligence and wit have supplied me with a grand view of the world which would never have been the same without you.

Love to all.

ACKNOWLEDGMENTS

Riley F. Uglum

I'm truly grateful to those whose guidance and wisdom made this book possible. There are so many who have influenced my life in positive ways.

My wife Kathy's support and counsel are a critical component in all of my endeavors. Michael E. Gerber awakened the entrepreneur within and taught me it was OK to dream bigger than I ever thought possible. Jon LoDuca expanded my mind in many ways and showed me how to package my experiential wisdom and share it with others.

Nelson Nash, Ray Poteet, Kim Butler and Todd Langford were instrumental in helping me learn the financial principles used by truly prosperous people. J. W. Vann is an exceptional optometrist and friend with whom I have had the pleasure of brainstorming with for a number of years. My son Brian and son-in-law Mat are the financial wizards of the family on whom I can rely to answer the tough "number crunching" questions. Lee Brower has helped me adapt a new and better perspective on life and how I can live mine in a worthwhile manner.

And many thanks to Dr. Kristy Bhend and the rest of my staff at Eye Care Associates of New Hampton for all of the amazing things they do.

Thank you to all others who have helped me along life's path and and whom are too numerous to mention here.

INTRODUCTION

Michael E. Gerber

As I write this book, the recession may have ended but it continues to take its toll on American businesses. Like any other industry, optometry is not immune from the downturn. Optometrists all over the country are watching as patients defer visits for eye and vision care. At a time when per-capita disposable income is at an all-time low, many people are choosing not to spend their hard-earned money on optometric services for themselves and even for their children. As a result, eye care moves from the realm of necessity to luxury, and regrettably, healthy vision becomes an expendable concern while industry revenue takes a sizeable dip into the red.

Faced with a struggling economy and fewer and fewer patients, many optometrists I've met are asking themselves, "Why did I ever become an optometrist in the first place?"

And it isn't just a money problem. After thirty-five years of working with small businesses, many of them optometry practices, I'm convinced that the dissatisfaction experienced by countless optometrists is not just about money. To be frank, the recession doesn't deserve all the blame, either. While the financial crisis our country is facing certainly hasn't made things any better, the problem started long before the economy tanked. Let's dig a little deeper. Let's go back to school.

Can you remember that far back? Whichever school or college of optometry you attended, you probably had some great teachers who helped you become the fine optometrist you are. These schools excel at teaching the science of optometry; they'll teach you everything you need to know about the eye, vision, pharmacology, and systemic diseases. But what they *don't* teach is the consummate skill set needed to be a successful optometrist, and they certainly don't teach what it takes to build a successful optometry enterprise.

Obviously, something is seriously wrong. The education that optometric professionals receive in school doesn't go far enough, deep enough, and broad enough. Schools of optometry don't teach you how to relate to the *enterprise* of optometry or to the *business* of optometry; they only teach you how to relate to the *practice* of optometry. In other words, they merely teach you how to be an *effective* rather than a *successful* optometrist. Last time I checked, they weren't offering ODs (doctor of optometry) in success.

That's why there are plenty of optometrists who are effective, but very few who are successful. Although a successful optometrist must be effective, an effective optometrist does not have to be—and in most cases isn't—successful.

An effective optometrist is capable of executing his or her duties with as much certainty and professionalism as possible.

A successful optometrist, on the other hand, works balanced hours, has little stress, leads rich and rewarding relationships with friends and family, and has an economic life that is diverse, fulfilling, and showing a continuous return on investment.

A successful optometrist finds time and ways to give back to the community but at little cost to his or her sense of ease.

A successful optometrist is a leader, someone who doesn't simply teach patients how to care for their eyes and protect their eyesight, but a sage; a rich person (in the broadest sense of the word); a strong father, mother, wife, or husband; a friend, teacher, mentor, and spiritually grounded human being; a person who can see clearly into all aspects of what it means to lead a fulfilling life.

So let's go back to the original question: Why did you become an optometrist? Were you striving to just be an effective one, or did you dream about real and resounding success?

I don't know how you've answered that question in the past, but I am confident that once you understand the strategic thinking laid out in this book, you will answer it differently in the future.

If the ideas here are going to be of value to you, it's critical that you begin to look at yourself in a different, more productive way. I am suggesting you go beyond the mere technical aspects of your daily job as an optometrist and begin instead to think strategically about your optometry practice as both a business and an enterprise.

I often say that most *practices* don't work—the people who own them do. In other words, most optometry practices are jobs for the optometrists who own them. Does this sound familiar? The optometrist, overcome by an entrepreneurial seizure, has started his or her own practice, become his or her own boss, and now works for a lunatic!

The result: the optometrist is running out of time, patience, and ultimately money. Not to mention paying the worst price anyone can pay for the inability to understand what a true practice is, what a true business is, and what a true enterprise is—the price of his or her life.

In this book I'm going to make the case for why you should think differently about what you do and why you do it. It isn't just the future of your optometry practice that hangs in the balance. It's the future of your life.

The E-Myth Optometrist is an exciting departure from my other sole-authored books. In this book Dr. Riley Uglum, an E-Myth expert—a licensed optometrist who has successfully applied the E-Myth to the development of his optometry practice—is sharing his secrets about how he achieved extraordinary results using the E-Myth paradigm. In addition to the time-tested E-Myth strategies and systems I'll be sharing with you, you'll benefit from the wisdom, guidance, and practical tips provided by Riley, who has been in your shoes.

The problems that afflict optometry practices today don't only exist in the field of medicine; the same problems are confronting every organization of every size in every industry in every country in the world. *The E-Myth Optometrist* is next in a new series of E-Myth expert books that will serve as a launching pad for Michael E. Gerber Partners™ to bring a legacy of expertise to small, struggling businesses in *all* industries. This series offers an exciting opportunity to understand and apply the significance of E-Myth methodology in both theory and practice to businesses in need of development and growth.

The E-Myth says that only by conducting your business in a truly innovative and independent way will you ever realize the unmatched joy that comes from creating a truly independent business, a business that works *without* you rather than *because* of you.

The E-Myth says that it is only by learning the difference between the work of a *business* and the business of *work* that optometrists will be freed from the predictable and often-overwhelming tyranny of the unprofitable, unproductive routine that consumes them on a daily basis.

The E-Myth says that what will make the ultimate difference between the success or failure of your optometry practice is first and foremost how you *think* about your business, as opposed to how hard you work in it.

So, let's think it through together. Let's think about those things—work, patients, money, time—that dominate the world of optometrists everywhere.

Let's talk about planning. About growth. About management. About getting a life!

Let's think about improving you and your family's life through the development of an extraordinary practice. About getting the life you've always dreamed of, but never thought you could actually have.

Envision the future you want, and the future is yours.

The Story of Steve and Peggy

Michael E. Gerber

You leave home to seek your fortune and, when you get it, you go home and share it with your family.

—Anita Baker

Every business is a family business. To ignore this truth is to court disaster.

I don't care if family members actually work in the business or not. Whatever his or her relationship with the business, every member of an optometrist's family will be greatly affected by the decisions an optometrist makes about the business. There's just no way around it.

Unfortunately, like most doctors, optometrists tend to compartmentalize their lives. They view their practice as a profession—what they do—and therefore none of their family's business.

"This has nothing to do with you," says the optometrist to his wife, with blind conviction. "I leave work at the office and family at home."

And with equal conviction, I say, "Not true!" In actuality, your family and optometry practice are inextricably linked to one

1

another. What's happening in your practice is also happening at home. Consider the following and ask yourself if each is true:

- If you're angry at work, you're also angry at home.
- If you're out of control in your optometry practice, you're equally out of control at home.
- If you're having trouble with money in your practice, you're also having trouble with money at home.
- If you have communication problems in your practice, you're also having communication problems at home.
- If you don't trust in your practice, you don't trust at home.
- If you're secretive in your practice, you're equally secretive at home.

And you're paying a huge price for it!

The truth is that your practice and your family are one—and you're the link. Or you should be. Because if you try to keep your practice and your family apart, if your practice and your family are strangers, you will effectively create two separate worlds that can never wholeheartedly serve each other. Two worlds that split each other apart.

Let me tell you the story of Steve and Peggy Walsh.

The Walshes met in college. They were lab partners in organic chemistry, Steve a pre-optometry student and Peggy pre-med. When their lab discussions started to wander beyond spectroscopy and carboxylic acids and into their personal lives, they discovered they had a lot in common. By the end of the course, they weren't just talking in class; they were talking on the phone every night . . . and *not* about orgo.

Steve thought Peggy was absolutely brilliant (her MCAT scores were off the charts), and Peggy considered Steve the most passionate man she knew. It wasn't long before they were engaged and planning their future together. A week after graduation, they were married in a lovely garden ceremony in Peggy's childhood home.

While Steve studied at a prestigious college of optometry, Peggy attended a prestigious medical school nearby. Over the next few years, the couple worked hard to keep their finances afloat. They worked long hours and studied constantly; they were often exhausted and struggled to make ends meet. But throughout it all, they were committed to what they were doing and to each other.

After passing the NBEO exam, Steve went on to get a specialized degree in ocular therapeutics while Peggy completed her residency. Then Steve started working for a large, publicly traded vision care company. Soon afterward, the couple had their first son, and Peggy decided to take some time off from the hospital to be with him. Those were good years. Steve and Peggy loved each other very much, were active members in their church, participated in community organizations, and spent quality time together. The Walshes considered themselves one of the most fortunate families they knew.

But work became troublesome. Steve grew increasingly frustrated with the way the company was run. "I want to go into business for myself," he announced one night at the dinner table. "I want to start my own practice."

Steve and Peggy spent many nights talking about the move. Was it something they could afford? Did Steve really have the skills necessary to make an optometry practice a success? Were there enough patients to go around? What impact would such a move have on Peggy's practice at the local hospital, their lifestyle, their son, their relationship? They asked all the questions they thought they needed to answer before Steve went into business for himself . . . but they never really drew up a concrete plan.

Finally, tired of talking and confident that he could handle whatever he might face, Steve committed to starting his own optometry practice. Because she loved and supported him, Peggy agreed, offering her own commitment to help in any way she could. So Steve quit his job, took out a second mortgage on their home, and leased a small office nearby.

In the beginning, things went well. A building boom had hit the town, and new families were pouring into the area. Steve had no trouble getting new patients. His practice expanded, quickly outgrowing his office.

Within a year, Steve had employed an office manager, Clarissa, to book appointments and handle the administrative side of the business. He also hired a bookkeeper, Tim, to handle the finances. Steve was ecstatic with the progress his young practice had made. He celebrated by taking his wife and son on vacation to Italy.

Of course, managing a business was more complicated and time-consuming than working for someone else. Steve not only supervised all the jobs Clarissa and Tim did, he was continually looking for work to keep everyone busy. When he wasn't scanning journals of optometry to stay abreast of what was going on in the field or fulfilling continuing-education requirements to stay current on the latest standards of care, he was going to the bank, wading through patient paperwork, or speaking with insurance companies (which usually degenerated into *arguing* with insurance companies). He also found himself spending more and more time on the telephone dealing with patient complaints and nurturing relationships.

As the months went by and more and more patients came through the door, Steve had to spend even more time just trying to keep his head above water.

By the end of its second year, the practice, now employing two full-time and two part-time people, had moved to a larger office downtown. The demands on Steve's time had grown with the practice.

He began leaving home earlier in the morning, returning home later at night. He drank more. He rarely saw his son anymore. For the most part, Steve was resigned to the problem. He saw the hard work as essential to building the "sweat equity" he had long heard about.

Money was also becoming a problem for Steve. Although the practice was growing like crazy, money always seemed scarce when it was really needed. He had discovered that insurance companies were often slow to pay.

When Steve had worked for somebody else, he had been paid twice a month. In his own practice, he often had to wait—sometimes for months. He was still owed money on billings he had completed more than 90 days before.

When he complained to late-paying insurers, it fell on deaf ears. They would shrug, smile, and promise to do their best, adding, "But you know how business is."

Of course, no matter how slowly Steve got paid, he still had to pay *his* people. This became a relentless problem. Steve often felt like a juggler dancing on a tightrope. A fire burned in his stomach day and night.

To make matters worse, Steve began to feel that Peggy was insensitive to his troubles. Not that he often talked to his wife about the practice. "Business is business" was Steve's mantra. "It's my responsibility to handle things at the office and Peggy's responsibility to take care of her own job and the family."

Peggy herself was working late hours at the hospital, and they'd brought in a nanny to help with their son. Steve couldn't help but notice that his wife seemed resentful, and her apparent lack of understanding baffled him. Didn't she see that he had a practice to take care of? That he was doing it all for his family? Apparently not.

As time went on, Steve became even more consumed and frustrated by his practice. When he went off on his own, he remembered saying, "I don't like people telling me what to do." But people were still telling him what to do. On one particularly frustrating morning, his office had to get an insurance authorization for a $37 glaucoma test. It required a long-distance call and twenty-five minutes on hold. Steve was furious.

Not surprisingly, Peggy grew more frustrated by her husband's lack of communication. She cut back on her own hours at the hospital to focus on their family, but her husband still never seemed to be around. Their relationship grew tense and strained. The rare moments they *were* together were more often than not peppered by long silences—a far cry from the heartfelt conversations that had characterized their relationship's early days, when they'd talk into the wee hours of the morning.

Meanwhile, Tim, the bookkeeper, was also becoming a problem for Steve. Tim never seemed to have the financial information Steve needed to make decisions about payroll, patient billing, and general operating expenses, let alone how much money was available for Steve and Peggy's living expenses.

When questioned, Tim would shift his gaze to his feet and say, "Listen, Steve, I've got a lot more to do around here than you can imagine. It'll take a little more time. Just don't press me, okay?"

Overwhelmed by his own work, Steve usually backed off. The last thing Steve wanted was to upset Tim and have to do the books himself. He could also empathize with what Tim was going through, given the practice's growth over the past year.

Late at night in his office, Steve would sometimes recall his first years out of school. He missed the simple life he and his family had shared. Then, as quickly as the thoughts came, they would vanish. He had work to do and no time for daydreaming. "Having my own practice is a great thing," he would remind himself. "I simply have to apply myself, as I did in school, and get on with the job. I have to work as hard as I always have when something needed to get done."

Steve began to live most of his life inside his head. He began to distrust his people. They never seemed to work hard enough or to care about his practice as much as he did. If he wanted to get something done, he usually had to do it himself.

Then one day, the office manager, Clarissa, quit in a huff, frustrated by the amount of work that her boss was demanding of her. Steve was left with a desk full of papers and a telephone that wouldn't stop ringing.

Clueless about the work Clarissa had done, Steve was overwhelmed by having to pick up the pieces of a job he didn't understand. His world turned upside down. He felt like a stranger in his own practice.

Why had he been such a fool? Why hadn't he taken the time to learn what Clarissa did in the office? Why had he waited until now?

Ever the trouper, Steve plowed into Clarissa's job with everything he could muster. What he found shocked him. Clarissa's work space was a disaster area! Her desk drawers were a jumble of papers, coins, pens, pencils, rubber bands, envelopes, business cards, contact lenses, eye drops, and candy.

"What was she thinking?" Steve raged.

When he got home that night, even later than usual, he got into a shouting match with Peggy. He settled it by storming out of the house to get a drink. Didn't anybody understand him? Didn't anybody care what he was going through?

He returned home only when he was sure Peggy was asleep. He slept on the couch and left early in the morning, before anyone was awake. He was in no mood for questions or arguments.

When Steve got to his office the next morning, he immediately headed for the medicine cabinet . . .

What lessons can we draw from Steve and Peggy's story? I've said it once and I'll say it again: every business is a family business. Your business profoundly touches every member of your family, even if they never set foot inside your office. Every business either gives to the family or takes from the family, just as individual family members do.

If the business takes, the family is always the first to pay the price.

In order for Steve to free himself from the prison he created, he would first have to admit his vulnerability. He would have to confess to himself and his family that he really doesn't know enough about his own practice and how to grow it.

Steve tried to do it all himself. Had he succeeded, had the practice supported his family in the style he imagined, he would have burst with pride. Instead, Steve unwittingly isolated himself, thereby achieving the exact opposite of what he sought.

He destroyed his life—and his family's life along with it.

Repeat after me: Every business is a family business.

Are you like Steve? I believe that all optometrists share a common soul with him. You must learn that a business is only a business. It is not your life. But it is also true that your business can have a profoundly negative impact on your life unless you learn how to do it differently than most optometrists do it—and definitely differently than Steve did it.

Steve's optometry practice could have served his and his family's life. But for that to happen, he would have had to learn how to master his practice in a way that was completely foreign to him.

Instead, Steve's practice consumed him. Because he lacked a true understanding of the essential strategic thinking that would have allowed him to create something unique, Steve and his family were doomed from day one.

This book contains the secrets that Steve should have known. If you follow in Steve's footsteps, prepare to have your life and business fall apart. But if you apply the principles we'll discuss here, you can avoid a similar fate.

In the next chapter, we will see how optometry became a family business for Riley and how E-Myth principles profoundly changed his life. ✤

The Story of Riley and Kathy

Riley F. Uglum

A man should never neglect his family for business.

—Walt Disney

Kathy and I were high school sweethearts. We met in our junior year of high school after Kathy's family moved to New Hampton, Iowa, from Waterloo, Iowa. We got married after my second year of optometry school. For the next three years, Kathy worked as a secretary in South Chicago while I finished my optometry training.

We had no money in those days and lived in a zero-bedroom apartment where we cooked, ate, slept, studied, watched TV, and bathed in a space the size of our master bedroom now. But we had friends in the same situation and actually enjoyed this simple lifestyle. There were no children or mortgages to be concerned with, and we always scraped together enough cash to go out for pizza on weekends, attend an occasional Chicago Blackhawks hockey game, or go to the horse track, where we would split $2 bets with our friends because we couldn't afford any more. And of course, my classmates and I knew that we would soon be doctors, living life on a grander scale while our spouses reaped the rewards of putting us through school by relaxing at home and raising our children.

As fourth-year optometry students, we all believed that to truly live "The Dream," we needed to own and manage our own optometry practice someday. We needed to be in charge of our own destinies and provide the unique and individualized patient care that could not exist in retail optometry working for a large corporation. The benefits of being our own bosses had been drilled into us from day one of our optometry training. Anything else was just a job. It's funny now looking back at how private practice ownership was touted as the only real way we could be fulfilled in the world of optometry, while absolutely no "real world" business skills were taught to help us support this dream.

After graduation, I signed a contract to work for my uncle, W.E. Tunnell, OD, in his practice, knowing that he would be phasing out in a few years. The business was in my hometown, where many people knew me, so obviously they would be lined up at the door eager to receive eye care from a newly minted OD that was so full of knowledge (and himself).

Well, a couple of months later, Kathy looked for a job to help us pay the rent. So much for her early retirement. I was seeing a few patients, but had no marketing plan in place to see more. I provided great care for these patients, but was fearful of charging them too much or asking them to pay their bills.

And then we started having children. I now realize that this is when the optometry business really became a family business for us. I didn't know it at the time, but years later, after listening to Michael E. Gerber talk about every business being a family business, it began to sink in. Kathy was torn between living her dream of staying at home and raising our kids, and continuing with her job to help us pay the bills. My lack of business skills, along with the desire to own my own business, was significantly impacting the quality of my family's life! Who would have guessed? I certainly didn't see this coming while I was doing my optometry training. And why would I? No one ever told me this is what could happen out there in the real world.

Fast-forward a few years. Kathy did quit her job and spent quality time with our children when they were infants and toddlers. And she helped care for my mother, who had a stroke during this period. It was a good thing that we were used to living simply, because I wasn't yet generating enough income to support a very lavish lifestyle. But I was slowly learning some business basics, and as my uncle phased out of the practice, I began seeing more patients. Yes, I was turning a significant corner in my career. And when I purchased the practice in the early 1980s, I transitioned from working for someone else to working for myself. And then, a few years later, I made the next transition—that of working for a lunatic—me. I never saw this one coming, either!

My lack of business skills made it impossible to manage the growth of my practice. I didn't have proper staffing, so I always ran behind. I worked long after closing time finishing charts, and in general became stressed out to the point that I hated the thought of going to work in the mornings. It wasn't long before Kathy went back to work—in my practice—and it truly became a family business.

Now we were both involved with the headaches of staff turnover, accounts receivable (AR), accounts payable (AP), third-party managed care plans, managing payroll, handling difficult patients, dealing with optical vendors and labs, working with the accountant, and all the other issues involved with running a small business. We always made time to go to our kids' functions even though it meant reducing our production by being out of the office. But we seldom took the time to have real vacations because of the cash-flow problems it would create. And as our children moved on from high school to college, I never mentioned or recommended optometry as a career choice. I just couldn't see a future in it for them.

As you can see, my poorly managed business affected our family in different ways and at different times, but the bottom line was that the family was always affected by the business. And this same scenario played out in most of my colleagues' businesses across the nation. Some of them handled the stress by trying to share it with another OD partner who also had limited business skills. More often than not, these partnerships created even more stress than a solo OD had and ended in disastrous breakups that affected their families financially, psychologically, and emotionally. Divorces, alcoholism, gambling problems, high staff turnover, and other afflictions were as much a problem for optometrists as they were for dentists, physicians, and just about anyone else operating as a small business in the health care arena.

I remembered at this time how I had felt sorry for the graduating ODs who had no private practice opportunities and needed to take a "job" in the corporate retail world. But at this point, I had created a "job" for myself with many more hours and much more stress than they had. I actually purchased a time management system that I thought would help relieve this stress, but found that I didn't have enough time to learn how to use it. Go figure!

Fortunately for me, the 1980s were a time when health care providers could run a business poorly and still survive. The environment was far more forgiving than it is today. There weren't many managed care plans and private-pay patients were the norm. And well-intentioned small business owners with poor business skills could make a decent living. Today's environment is completely different. If I were to do the same things today that I did twenty-five years ago, my business would fail. The learning curve for building a small health care-based business is much steeper now. And although optometry schools teach excellent clinical skills, they aren't enough to allow a new graduate to survive (let alone thrive) on his or her own as we head into the second decade of the 21st century.

And what about those optometrists who are struggling to maintain their private practices now in the face of oppressive managed care plans and heavily discounted retail optical competition? Is there any hope that they can turn things around?

I believe the answer to that question is yes, as long as they have a sincere desire to do so. In my case, that desire was born of the misery that my practice had created for myself and my family. I possessed no special business skills, but thanks to the wisdom contained in *The E-Myth Revisited*, I began to understand how I might be able to completely transform my life if I dedicated myself to a serious entrepreneurial training program.

I will be eternally grateful that I was able to learn the skills necessary to transform my practice into a recession-proof business that grows in good economies and bad. I'm grateful that I learned to shift my focus from clinical care to the strategic work that allowed my business to grow into an enterprise. I'm grateful that Kathy and I are free to do meaningful work as entrepreneurs and make a difference in the lives of others. I'm grateful that I was able to provide a wonderful career opportunity for Dr. Kristy Bhend. I'm grateful for the great chemistry that has been created with my staff and for the unique care that we provide for our patients.

The E-Myth philosophy states that the reason a business exists is to enhance the lives of everyone who comes in contact with it. And *wow*, my business now exemplifies that philosophy. Fun stuff! ✤

CHAPTER 3

On the Subject of Money

Michael E. Gerber

There are three faithful friends: an old wife, an old dog, and ready money.

—Benjamin Franklin

Had Steve and Peggy first considered the subject of *money* as we will here, their lives could have been radically different. Money is on the tip of every optometrist's tongue, on the edge (or at the very center) of every optometrist's thoughts, intruding on every part of an optometrist's life.

With money consuming so much energy, why do so few optometrists handle it well? Why was Steve, like so many optometrists, willing to entrust his financial affairs to a relative stranger? Why is money scarce for most optometrists? Why is there less money than expected? And yet the demand for money is *always* greater than anticipated.

What is it about money that is so elusive, so complicated, so difficult to control? Why is it that every optometrist I've ever met hates to deal with the subject of money? Why are they almost always too late in facing money problems? And why are they constantly obsessed with the desire for more of it?

Money—you can't live with it and you can't live without it. But you better understand it and get your people to understand it. Because until you do, money problems will eat your practice for lunch.

You don't need an accountant or financial planner to do this. You simply need to prod your people to relate to money very personally. From optician to receptionist, they should all understand the financial impact of what they do every day in relationship to the profit and loss of the practice.

And so you must teach your people to think like owners, not like opticians or office managers or receptionists. You must teach them to operate like personal profit centers, with a sense of how their work fits in with the practice as a whole.

You must involve everyone in the practice with the topic of money—how it works, where it goes, how much is left, and how much everybody gets at the end of the day. You also must teach them about the four kinds of money created by the practice.

The Four Kinds of Money

In the context of owning, operating, developing, and exiting from an optometry practice, money can be split into four distinct but highly integrated categories:

- Income
- Profit
- Flow
- Equity

Failure to distinguish how the four kinds of money play out in your practice is a surefire recipe for disaster.

Important note: Do not talk to your accountants or bookkeepers about what follows; it will only confuse them and you.

The information comes from the real-life experiences of thousands of small business owners, optometrists included, most of whom were hopelessly confused about money when I met them. Once they understood and accepted the following principles, they developed a clarity about money that could only be called enlightened.

The First Kind of Money: Income

Income is the money optometrists are paid by their practice for doing their job *in* the practice. It's what they get paid for going to work every day.

Clearly, if optometrists didn't do their job, others would have to, and *they* would be paid the money the practice currently pays the optometrists. Income, then, has nothing to do with *ownership*. Income is solely the province of *employee-ship*.

That's why to the optometrist-as-*employee*, Income is the most important form money can take. To the optometrist-as-*owner*, however, it is the least important form money can take.

Most important; least important. Do you see the conflict? The conflict between the optometrist-as-employee and the optometrist-as-owner?

We'll deal with this conflict later. For now, just know that it is potentially the most paralyzing conflict in an optometrist's life.

Failing to resolve this conflict will cripple you. Resolving it will set you free.

The Second Kind of Money: Profit

Profit is what's left over after an optometry practice has done its job effectively and efficiently. If there is no profit, the practice is doing something wrong.

However, just because the practice shows a profit does not mean it is necessarily doing all the right things in the right way. Instead, it just means that something was done right during or preceding the period in which the profit was earned.

The important issue here is whether the profit was intentional or accidental. If it happened by accident (which most profit does), don't take credit for it. You'll live to regret your impertinence.

If it happened intentionally, take all the credit you want. You've earned it. Because profit created intentionally, rather than by accident, is replicable—again and again. And your practice's ability to repeat its performance is the most critical ability it can have.

As you'll soon see, the value of money is a function of your practice's ability to produce it in predictable amounts at an above-average return on investment.

Profit can be understood only in the context of your practice's purpose, as opposed to *your* purpose as an optometrist. Profit, then, fuels the forward motion of the practice that produces it. This is accomplished in four ways:

- Profit is *investment capital* that feeds and supports growth.
- Profit is *bonus capital* that rewards people for exceptional work.
- Profit is *operating capital* that shores up money shortfalls.
- Profit is *return-on-investment* capital that rewards you, the optometrist-owner, for taking risks.

Without profit, an optometry practice cannot subsist, much less grow. Profit is the fuel of progress.

If a practice misuses or abuses profit, however, the penalty is much like having no profit at all. Imagine the plight of an optometrist who has way too much return-on-investment capital and not enough investment capital, bonus capital, and operating capital. Can you see the imbalance this creates?

The Third Kind of Money: Flow

Flow is what money *does* in an optometry practice, as opposed to what money *is*. Whether the practice is large or small, money tends to move erratically through it, much like a pinball. One minute it's there; the next minute it's not.

Flow can be even more critical to a practice's survival than profit, because a practice can produce a profit and still be short of money. Has this ever happened to you? It's called profit on paper rather than in fact.

No matter how large your practice, if the money isn't there when it's needed, you're threatened—regardless of how much profit you've made. You can borrow it, of course. But money acquired in dire circumstances is almost always the most expensive kind of money you can get.

Knowing where the money is and where it will be when you need it is a critically important task of both the optometrist-as-employee and the optometrist-as-owner.

Rules of Flow

You will learn no lesson more important than the huge impact flow can have on the health and survival of your optometry practice, let alone your business or enterprise. The following two rules will help you understand why this subject is so critical.

1. **The First Rule of Flow states that your income statement is static, while the flow is dynamic.** Your income statement is a snapshot, while the flow is a moving picture. So, while your income statement is an excellent tool for analyzing your practice *after* the fact, it's a poor tool for managing it in the heat of the moment.

Your income statement tells you (1) how much money you're spending and where, and (2) how much money you're receiving and from where.

Flow gives you the same information as the income statement, plus it tells you *when* you're spending and receiving money. In other words, flow is an income statement moving through time. And that is the key to understanding flow. It is about management in real time. How much is coming in? How much is going out? You'd like to know this daily, or even by the hour if possible. Never by the week or month.

You must be able to forecast flow. You must have a flow plan that helps you gain a clear vision of the money that's out there next month and the month after that. You must also pinpoint what your needs will be in the future.

Ultimately, however, when it comes to flow, the action is always in the moment. It's about *now*. The minute you start to meander away from the present, you'll miss the boat.

Unfortunately, few optometrists pay any attention to flow until it dries up completely and slow pay becomes no pay. They are oblivious to this kind of detail until, say, patients announce that they won't pay for this or that. That gets an optometrist's attention because the expenses keep on coming.

When it comes to flow, most optometrists are flying by the proverbial seat of their pants. No matter how many people you hire to take care of your money, until you change the way you think about it, you will always be out of luck. No one can do this for you.

Managing flow takes attention to detail. But when flow is managed, your life takes on an incredible sheen. You're swimming with the current, not against it. You're in charge!

1. **The Second Rule of Flow states that money seldom moves as you expect it to.** But you do have the power to change that, provided you understand the two primary sources of money as it comes in and goes out of your optometry practice.

The truth is, the more control you have over the *source* of money, the more control you have over its flow. The sources of money are both inside and outside of your practice.

Money comes from *outside* your practice in the form of receivables, reimbursements, investments, and loans.

Money comes from *inside* your practice in the form of payables, taxes, capital investments, and payroll. These are the costs associated with attracting patients, delivering your services, operations, and so forth.

Few optometrists see the money going *out* of their practice as a source of money, but it is.

When considering how to spend money in your practice, you can save—and therefore make—money in three ways:

- Do it more effectively.
- Do it more efficiently.
- Stop doing it altogether.

By identifying the money sources inside and outside of your practice, and then applying these methods, you will be immeasurably better at controlling the flow in your practice

But what are these sources? They include how you:

- Manage your services
- Buy supplies and equipment
- Compensate your people
- Plan people's use of time
- Determine the direct cost of your services
- Increase the time you spend seeing patients
- Manage your work
- Collect reimbursements and receivables

And countless more. In fact, every task performed in your practice (and ones you haven't yet learned how to perform) can be done more efficiently and effectively, dramatically reducing the cost of doing business. In the process, you will create more income, produce more profit, and balance the flow.

The Fourth Kind of Money: Equity

Sadly, few optometrists fully appreciate the value of equity in their optometry practice. Yet, equity is the second most valuable asset any optometrist will ever possess. (The first most valuable asset is, of course, your life. More on that later.)

Equity is the financial value placed on your optometry practice by a prospective buyer.

Thus, your *practice* is your most important product, not your services. Because your practice has the power to set you free. That's right. Once you sell your practice—providing you get what you want for it—you're free!

Of course, to enhance your equity, to increase your practice's value, you have to build it right. You have to build a practice that works. A practice that can become a true business, and a business that can become a true enterprise. A practice/business/enterprise that can produce income, profit, flow, and equity better than any other optometrist's practice can.

To accomplish that, your practice must be designed so that it can do what it does systematically and predictably, every single time.

The Story of McDonald's

Let me tell you the most unlikely story anyone has ever told you about the successful building of an optometry practice, business, and enterprise. Let me tell you the story of Ray Kroc.

You might be thinking, "What on earth does a hamburger stand have to do with my practice? I'm not in the hamburger business; I'm an optometrist."

Yes, you are. But by practicing optometry as you have been taught, you've abandoned any chance to expand your reach, help more patients, or improve your services the way they must be improved if the practice of optometry—and your life—is going to be transformed.

In Ray Kroc's story lies the answer.

Ray Kroc called his first McDonald's restaurant "a little money machine." That's why thousands of franchises bought it. And the reason it worked? Ray Kroc demanded consistency, so that a hamburger in Philadelphia would be an advertisement for one in Peoria. In fact, no matter where you bought a McDonald's hamburger in the 1950s, the meat patty was guaranteed to weigh exactly 1.6 ounces, with a diameter of 3⅝ inches. It was in the McDonald's handbook.

Did Ray Kroc succeed? You know he did! And so can you, once you understand his methods. Consider just one part of Ray Kroc's story.

In 1954, Ray Kroc made his living selling the five-spindle Multimixer milkshake machine. He heard about a hamburger stand in San Bernardino, Calif., that had eight of his machines in operation, meaning it could make 40 shakes simultaneously. This he had to see.

Kroc flew from Chicago to Los Angeles, then drove 60 miles to San Bernardino. As he sat in his car outside Mac and Dick McDonald's restaurant, he watched as lunch customers lined up for bags of hamburgers.

In a revealing moment, Kroc approached a strawberry blonde in a yellow convertible. As he later described it, "It was not her sex appeal but the obvious relish with which she devoured the hamburger that made my pulse begin to hammer with excitement."

Passion.

In fact, it was the french fry that truly captured his heart. Before the 1950s, it was almost impossible to buy fries of consistent quality. Ray Kroc changed all that. "The french fry," he once wrote, "would become almost sacrosanct for me, its preparation a ritual to be followed religiously."

Passion and preparation.

The potatoes had to be just so—top-quality Idaho russets, 8 ounces apiece, deep-fried to a golden brown, and salted with a shaker that, as Kroc put it, kept going "like a Salvation Army girl's tambourine."

As Kroc soon learned, potatoes too high in water content—and even top-quality Idaho russets varied greatly in water content—will come out soggy when fried. And so Kroc sent out teams of workers, armed with hydrometers, to make sure all his suppliers were producing potatoes in the optimal solids range of 20 to 23 percent.

Preparation and passion. Passion and preparation. Look those words up in the dictionary and you'll see Ray Kroc's picture. Can you envision your picture there?

Do you understand what Ray Kroc did? Do you see why he was able to sell thousands of franchises? Kroc knew the true value of equity, and, unlike Steve from our story, Kroc went to work *on* his business rather than *in* his business. He knew the hamburger wasn't his product—McDonald's was!

So what does *your* optometry practice need to do to become a little money machine? What is the passion that will drive you to build a practice that works—a turnkey system like Ray Kroc's?

Equity and the Turnkey System

What's a turnkey system? And why is it so valuable to you? To better understand it, let's look at another example of a turnkey system that worked to perfection: the recordings of Frank Sinatra.

Frank Sinatra's records were to him as McDonald's restaurants were to Ray Kroc. They were part of a turnkey system that allowed Sinatra to sing to millions of people without having to be there himself.

Sinatra's recordings were a dependable turnkey system that worked predictably, systematically, automatically, and effortlessly to produce the same results every single time—no matter where they were played, and no matter who was listening.

Regardless of where Frank Sinatra was, his records just kept on producing income, profit, flow, and equity, over and over . . . and still do! Sinatra needed only to produce the prototype recording and the system did the rest.

Kroc's McDonald's is another prototypical turnkey solution, addressing everything McDonald's needs to do in a basic, systematic way so that anyone properly trained by McDonald's can successfully reproduce the same results.

And this is where you'll realize your equity opportunity: in the way your practice does business; in the way your practice systematically does what you intend it to do; and in the development of your turnkey system—a system that works even in the hands of ordinary people (and optometrists less experienced than you) to produce extraordinary results.

Remember:

- If you want to build vast equity in your practice, then go to work *on* your practice, building it into a business that works every single time.

- Go to work *on* your practice to build a totally integrated turnkey system that delivers exactly what you promised every single time.

- Go to work *on* your practice to package it and make it stand out from the optometry practices you see everywhere else.

Here is the most important idea you will ever hear about your practice and what it can potentially provide for you:

The value of your equity is directly proportional to how well your practice works. And how well your practice works is directly proportional to the effectiveness of the systems you have put into place upon which the operation of your practice depends.

Whether money takes the form of income, profit, flow, or equity, the amount of it—and how much of it stays with you— invariably boils down to this. Money, happiness, life—it all depends on how well your practice works. Not on your people, not on you, but on the system.

Your practice holds the secret to more money. Are you ready to learn how to find it?

Earlier in this chapter, I alerted you to the inevitable conflict between the optometrist-as-employee and the optometrist-as-owner. It's a battle between the part of you working *in* the practice and the part of you working *on* the practice. Between the part of you working for income and the part of you working for equity.

Here's how to resolve this conflict:

1. Be honest with yourself about whether you're filling *employee* shoes or *owner* shoes.

2. As your practice's key employee, determine the most effective way to do the job you're doing, *and then document that job.*

3. Once you've documented the job, create a strategy for replacing yourself with someone else (another optometrist, or, even better, a technician) who will then use your documented system exactly as you do.

4. Have your new employees manage the newly delegated system. Improve the system by quantifying its effectiveness over time.

5. Repeat this process throughout your practice wherever you catch yourself acting as employee rather than owner.

6. Learn to distinguish between ownership work and employee-ship work every step of the way.

Master these methods, understand the difference between the four kinds of money, develop an interest in how money works in your practice … and then watch it flow in with the speed and efficiency of LASIK.

Now let's take another step in our strategic thinking process. Let's look at the subject of *planning*. But first, let's see how a better understanding of money has helped Riley with his optometry business. ✤

CHAPTER
4

Money Dynamics– Seeing Is Believing

Riley F. Uglum

Money is in some respects life's fire: it is a very excellent servant, but a terrible master.

—P.T. Barnum

Why do you suppose this chapter on money appears so early in the book? It's because without money, the rest of the chapters are meaningless. It's really that simple. There is absolutely no need to write a chapter on strategically leveraging people when we have no money to pay them. Nor is the chapter on growth necessary when there is no money to capitalize that growth. Money, or lack thereof, is the primary reason that an optometry practice (or any business, for that matter) fails.

Optometrists' clinical abilities are important to their success as private practitioners, but they must be combined with solid money skills if they wish to prosper. Unfortunately, most optometrists have no understanding of money when they graduate from optometry school. It simply isn't part of the curriculum.

Where, then, does the average OD acquire the financial wisdom to stay in business? For me, the answers came from multiple sources. Early in my career, I took some basic accounting courses and used various consultants who helped me to learn the fundamentals of finance. But what really allowed me to grow and thrive in my practice were two things:

- E-Myth Mastery education
- Advanced entity structuring and prosperity economic principles

The effect of these two discoveries on my business and personal life were so profound that I started a company, Promethean Ventures, whose mission is to teach them to other optometrists. So let's take a look at them in more detail.

E-Myth Mastery taught me the four major dynamics of money and how they affect a small business. They are:

- Income
- Profit
- Flow
- Equity

From my prosperity economics education, I learned that there are other factors that can have a dramatic effect on these four money dynamics. They are:

- The structure of our business entity environment
- Opportunity cost
- Access to capital

Let's take a look at how they work.

Income and Profit—What's the Difference?

When I finally started seeing a sufficient number of patients that helped me actually meet all of my living expenses and have some money left over at the end of the year, it was like being in seventh heaven. I took a monthly draw during the year, which took care of most personal expenses. Then, as December 31 arrived, it was exciting to see how much profit would be left over to bonus out (to me) as more income. There was no distinction between me as the employee OD and the business owner OD. There was no distinction between income and profits. Why should there be? Left pocket or right pocket—who cares? The pockets were both mine, and that was all that mattered. I was finally getting some "payback" for that expensive optometry education.

But let's assume for a moment that I was working for another business. Would that business owner take all of his profit for the year and give it to me, his employee OD? And if he did, would he be able to remain in business for the long haul? The answer to both these questions is a resounding *no!*

So I began to understand that owner profits *were not* the same as employee income. A separation of employee and owner roles was necessary. As the business owner, I needed to have a profit left over after paying rent, utilities, vendors, staff, etc., *and* after paying myself as an employee OD. This separation seemed weird at first. What was I worth as an employee? How much should I pay an employee OD? Would this separation affect my lifestyle?

I also began to realize that equipment purchases and other capital expenditures needed to be based on sound business strategies. Before this, such decisions were haphazard and tempered by how my end-of-year income might be affected. Or sometimes it was an accountant's recommendation to buy some equipment to get the end-of-year tax deductions. In any case, it was "seat of the pants" management with no overall strategic plan. I hadn't yet made the separation between profits and income.

It wasn't difficult to *determine* what employee ODs were paid per year. So I just started writing monthly paychecks for that amount and considered it my income. At the end of the year, I put on my business owner's hat (instead of my employee hat) and considered what to do with the business profits. There were four E-myth ways that I could allocate them, and another way that involved prosperity economic strategies.

The E-Myth Profit Allocation Strategies:

1. Use the profit to fuel practice growth (investment capital) with measurable return on investment (ROI) by:

   - Purchasing new equipment
   - Investing in staff training and education
   - Investing in new products and services
   - Improving marketing strategies
   - Recruiting quality staff
   - Upgrading the facility to improve the sensory package
   - Expanding the facility to support more services/products

2. Use the profit for bonus capital to reward exceptional work. Bonuses increase staff morale, which has its own return on investment in the form of happy patients that refer other patients.

3. Use the profit as a reserve to avoid cash-flow problems.

4. Allocate the profit as return-on-investment capital for me, the OD business owner, as a reward for taking the risks involved with owning a business.

By selecting only the fourth option, I could continue to selfishly take most of the excess profit as return-on-investment capital if I wished. Or, I could consciously weigh the other options and choose to use some of those profits to grow my business.

The Prosperity Economics Profit Allocation Options:

1. Reallocate owner return-on-investment profit (and even some OD employee W-2 dollars) to an outsourcing company owned by an owner OD's family. This company could perform various services such as equipment leasing, optical management, bookkeeping, marketing, AR/AP

management, etc. The outsourcing company could then use these dollars for:

- A family health plan—including insurance premiums
- College tuition expenses
- Cars, computers, cell phones, and other necessary business expenses
- Equipment purchases (for leaseback to the optometry practice)
- A cash reserve (in a much more favorable tax environment)

2. Use profit to fund family banking systems for all employees (including the owners) in lieu of qualified plan contributions. This strategy has the following advantages:

   - It builds a retirement plan with significant advantages over traditional qualified plans.
   - It creates a personal banking system that can be used by employees to finance cars, vacations, home improvements, college tuition, or just about anything they might otherwise use credit cards or traditional financing for.
   - It can be used by a family-owned outsourcing company to purchase equipment that is then leased back to the practice.
   - The practice can borrow funds directly from the system for inexpensive access to capital.
   - All finance charges go back into the personal economic and retirement plan of the employees or owners to be used again and again.

In my case, I have been able to reduce my W-2 wages significantly using the above strategies without affecting my lifestyle whatsoever. This frees up more cash to hire more staff and grow my business. Wise allocation of profit really requires a strategic growth plan, which is a different subject and will be addressed in the next chapter.

Income and Profits with Multiple ODs

When your practice grows to the point that you begin looking for an associate OD, the difference between income and profit becomes even more important. An employee OD receives income only. My philosophy is to pay associates a percentage of their actual production based on a twelve-month rolling net. In this way, they pay their fair share of the overhead and give up a percentage of their net to the owner for allocation according to E-Myth and/or prosperity economic principles.

They receive compensation much greater than the average OD because they are able to use well-tested systems that generate high-level production metrics. So it's a win-win situation for owner and associate. Actually it's a win-win-win-win situation because patients and staff are also beneficiaries in this type of practice.

I should also mention the importance of business structure when it comes to hiring another OD. Traditionally, an associate optometrist is hired as a W-2 employee by the owner OD's entity. This means taxes are deducted from the employee OD's paycheck, and that the owner pays matching Social Security and Medicare taxes. For an associate OD earning $96,000 annually, the owner pays about $8,000 in matching taxes every year. These are dollars that could be better allocated to business growth.

But if the new OD sets up his or her own business entity, the employer OD now pays another business for its services and has no matching taxes to contend with. Also, the associate OD now receives the full amount of compensation into his or her entity with absolutely no taxes being withheld. Such associates can now choose to allocate what they wish to spend on deductible, pre-tax items like a corporate health plan, computers, cell phones, car, business trips, etc. And of course they would take some W-2 wages, too.

But can you see how this arrangement is also win-win? The senior OD gets an associate more economically while the associate maintains a lifestyle better than what he or she would have with the W-2 employee arrangement. This type of entity structure is very basic, but it is the foundation upon which more sophisticated strategies can be developed.

When a new OD becomes a partner/owner, that person receives income commensurate to the time the associate works in the practice, and his or her share of any return-on-investment profits that are allocated. When a new partner buys into the practice, the purchase price is completely dependent on what the practice's equity is appraised at. A new buyer will certainly pay more for a thriving, growing business. And the seller will reap the just rewards for building such an attractive business. So let's look at how we might affect our practice's equity, which just happens to be another of the E-Myth's money dynamics.

Equity

I'm going to skip the flow of money for the moment. It will be discussed shortly. But while the subject of profit allocation is still fresh in our minds, please understand that if that allocation is done wisely, the equity of the business appreciates dramatically. And this equity is what ultimately determines how financially independent we may become.

Appreciated equity can be leveraged into financial freedom by selling it, either in portions or in its entirety. As emphasized previously, a thriving business is worth much more to a buyer than a stagnant one, especially if that business has documented systems that allow the new owner to get up to speed quickly.

So how do we allocate profits to build equity? One of the best ways is to invest in the development of solid business systems. Why do suppose a McDonald's franchise sells easily and for a premium price? It's because its systems have been carefully developed and proven to work time and time again.

Most doctors will tell you that McDonald's strategies won't work in health care because the nature of the two businesses is completely different. But this is completely untrue. I know, because my practice is doing it. Our key systems are not only written down, but many are video-documented and available on a website that can be viewed by our doctors and staff 24/7. So doctor/staff training can now be done more efficiently, even at 10 p.m. from home. It no longer requires intensive time commitments by senior staff for hands-on training, although some of that is still necessary.

We all know how disruptive it can be when a key employee leaves or can't work for an extended period of time. If what such employees do resides in their heads, you may never be able to replace their wisdom completely. But if what they do is completely systemized, you simply need to find another talented staff member to run their systems. So the business becomes systems-dependent rather than people-dependent.

And think of this from a doctor's perspective. In the event of death or disability, the practice equity is worth much more to prospective buyers if they know that your systems are accurately documented and that they can learn to run them without you being there. What more attractive opportunity could a buyer ask for than a turnkey, McDonald's-type operation? This is the type of business that buyers will pay a premium to own.

So we can see that allocating profits to build equity by investing in systems is a very sound business strategy.

The Flow of Money

Cash flow ultimately determines the success of a business. A great business can generate tons of sales, but unless those sales are accompanied by cash, a check, or a credit card swipe, it becomes difficult to pay staff, vendors, or the employee OD, let alone the owner. And you can forget allocating profits to fuel business growth, because there won't be any cash to allocate.

Before E-Myth, my practice suffered from poor cash-flow problems at least twice a year. And it wasn't because we weren't profitable or managing our accounts receivable correctly.

Ironically, my flow problems often resulted from having *too much cash!* No, I'm not using recreational drugs as I write this. Let me tell you how mismanagement of *opportunity cost* can create flow problems.

When my practice had a hefty cash reserve, I often paid for new equipment or a business vehicle in cash to avoid leasing or financing costs. This then resulted in a negative cash flow for a period of months, as there were no reserve funds for paying lab bills, payroll, and other vendors. And there was certainly no way I could take time off during this period. I needed to work hard to generate more cash to cover the negative flow. But I always thought I was doing the right thing by paying cash for larger purchases as long as the money was in the checking account. That's because I didn't understand opportunity cost yet.

The same thing happened when we paid out our six-month staff bonuses. These bonuses could be sizable because they were based on a percentage of the increase in profits over the previous year. The cash reserve was usually sufficient to cover the bonus, so the check was written. But in addition to the bonus, my business also had all of the other expenses created at the end of a major accounting period. And those checks were written, too, thus exacerbating the cash-flow problems.

So guess what usually happened? I held my own paycheck for a month or more until there was a sufficient balance in the business checking account to cash it. How frustrating—my business was profitable on the profit and loss statement, but I couldn't even cash my own paychecks. This is what happens when we mismanage flow and don't understand opportunity cost.

Some of my flow solutions were simple, such as waiting a couple of weeks to pay out a bonus or using pre-existing lines of credit with favorable rates. Other solutions required the use of opportunity cost strategies that had a very significant positive impact on my business and personal finances.

Opportunity Cost

When we pay for something in cash, we lose the opportunity it could provide us as:

- A cash reserve
- An income source (i.e. the return it could provide us if invested at a given rate of return)

I always thought "I had arrived" when I was able to purchase a new car with cash and no longer needed outside financing. Let's look at the heavy opportunity cost incurred by doing this. (The following calculator is courtesy of Todd Langford, president of Truth Concepts.)

We will assume the following:

- An account of $100,000 (in a business entity or personally)
- Annual rate of return of 7 percent
- Annual additions to the account of $12,000
- A car is purchased with cash every three years for $25,000 plus trade-in
- A thirty-year time frame (ten cars purchased for $250,000 in cash)

First, here is what the account looks like if no cars are purchased at all:

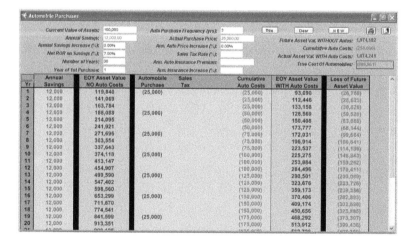

In the upper right-hand corner, we see that the account would grow to $1,974,102. Now let's see how purchasing a car with cash every three years for $25,000 changes things.

The actual cost of the cars paid in cash was $250,000, but we can see that the true cost (the opportunity cost lost by not earning 7 percent on that cash) was $899,861! Our account dropped from almost $2 million to $1,074,241! Consider that most optometrists own two or more cars for most of their lives and purchase expensive equipment for their practices on a regular basis. Do you see how important opportunity cost is?

Controlling Opportunity Cost

We finance everything we buy. We either pay interest charges to someone else for the use of that person's money, or we lose the opportunity cost of that money as just illustrated. This raises the question: *Is there any other way to do it?* And the answer is *absolutely!*

Promethean Ventures teaches cutting-edge financial principles to optometrists so that they can better manage the money dynamics of their practice. Reducing opportunity cost is a key Promethean strategy. Here is how we do it:

- Set up a properly structured personal banking system (like prosperous people do).
- Set up a family-owned leasing company.
- The leasing company borrows funds from the family bank to purchase equipment.
- The practice leases equipment from the leasing company.

  Opportunity cost is significantly reduced because:

- The family bank earns an internal return on the funds it lends in addition to the interest paid back by the leasing company.
- Interest payments incurred by the practice and the leasing company are deductible.

- Finance charges and interest payments are not lost to outside institutions.

Additionally, expensive equipment is now held in an entity that is protected from any lawsuits or judgments against the OD's practice. The funds in the personal banking system are also asset-protected, and they grow in a tax-deferred environment. Due to the unique nature of the financial vehicle Promethean uses, most of the dollars in the personal banking system can be withdrawn tax-free at retirement time—instead of being taxed like a traditional IRA or 401(k).

Promethean Ventures has used this strategy with practices of all sizes. Young practice owners start out financing smaller purchases and work up to larger ones. Mature ODs can begin with major equipment purchases the first year they start. And the personal banking system has actually replaced the traditional retirement plan we offer to our staff because of the significant additional advantages it provides for them.

Access to Capital

All business growth requires capital as its fuel. In optometry, money is required to pay doctors and staff, recruit quality doctors and staff, buy equipment, build or remodel facilities, purchase inventory, fund continuing education, and on and on. Capital can be obtained from outside sources if our credit ratings are good. But this capital carries a price tag and can be expensive.

It was demonstrated earlier in this chapter how an outsourcing company saves tax dollars, which can then be used for the capital needs of the business. So this strategy provides access to capital very inexpensively.

I also described a personal banking system that could be used to finance capital purchases for the practice while avoiding the opportunity costs of paying cash. Again, this strategy provides access to capital without the cost of using outside sources.

There is no better way to fund business growth than having readily available and inexpensive access to capital. This is how wealthy and prosperous people become more wealthy and prosperous. They create and grow businesses using "cheap money" to fuel that growth.

Summary

Understanding and systemizing the money aspects of my optometry practice was how it all started for me. It enabled me to transform my practice into a business that is now on its way to becoming an enterprise. And I can now feel what it is like to be an entrepreneur rather than living the "entrepreneurial myth."

You can do it, too. The money systems for optometry are already in place and ready to use for those who are ready to break out of the "doing it, doing it, doing it" grind. And these money systems are the perfect place to begin your entrepreneurial awakening.

New Promethean Ventures clients often comment on the unusual nature of the financial strategies we use. I wondered about them too when I was first introduced to them because they are non-traditional. However, I noticed that the people who were teaching them were all extremely successful and prosperous. Stop and think about how many wealthy people you know that say things like "I made all of my money with my mutual funds," or "My 401(k) was the key to my success."

I now have the privilege of networking with many prosperous entrepreneurs, and although they all use equity markets and real estate to their advantage, they attribute their true prosperity to building successful entrepreneurial businesses that use some form of these "non-traditional" financial concepts. For the average optometrist, it's really just a case of "You don't know what you don't know." So why not expand your entrepreneurial wisdom and experience the freedom to live life on your terms? It all starts with attaining the "money wisdom" necessary to build your practice into a business and then an enterprise. ❧

On the Subject of Planning

Michael E. Gerber

Luck is good planning, carefully executed.

—Anonymous

Another obvious oversight revealed in Steve and Peggy's story was the absence of true planning.

Every optometrist starting his or her own practice must have a plan. You should never begin to see patients without a plan in place. But, like Steve, most optometrists do exactly that.

An optometrist lacking a vision is simply someone who goes to work every day. Someone who is just doing it, doing it, doing it. Busy, busy, busy. Maybe making money, maybe not. Maybe getting something out of life, maybe not. Taking chances without really taking control.

The plan tells anyone who needs to know *how we do things here.* The plan defines the objective and the process by which you will attain it. The plan encourages you to organize tasks into functions, and then helps people grasp the logic of each of those functions. This in turn permits you to bring new employees up to speed quickly.

There are numerous books and seminars on the subject of practice management, but they focus on making you a better optometrist. I want to teach you something that you've never been taught before: how to be a manager. It has nothing to do with conventional practice management and everything to do with thinking like an entrepreneur.

The Planning Triangle

As we discussed in the Preface, every optometry practice is a company, every optometry business is a company, and every optometry enterprise is a company. Yet the difference between the three is extraordinary. Although all three may offer optometric services, how they do what they do is completely different.

The trouble with most companies owned by optometrists is that they are dependent on the optometrist. That's because they're a practice—the smallest, most limited form a company can take. Practices are formed around the technician, whether optometrist or roofer.

You may choose in the beginning to form a practice, but you should understand its limitations. The company called a *practice* depends on the owner—that is, the optometrist. The company called a *business* depends on other people plus a system by which that business does what it does. Once your practice becomes a business, you can replicate it, turning it into an *enterprise*.

Is your optometry company going to be a practice, a business, or an enterprise? Planning is crucial to answering this all-important question. Whatever you choose to do must be communicated by your plan, which is really three interrelated plans in one. We call it the Planning Triangle, and it consists of:

- The business plan
- The practice plan
- The completion plan

The three plans form a triangle, with the business plan at the base, the practice plan in the center, and the completion plan at the apex.

The business plan determines *who* you are (the business), the practice plan determines *what* you do (the specific focus of your optometry practice), and the completion plan determines *how* you do it (the fulfillment process).

By looking at the Planning Triangle, we see that the three critical plans are interconnected. The connection between them is established by asking the following questions:

1. Who are we?
2. What do we do?
3. How do we do it?

Who are we? is purely a strategic question.

What do we do? is both a strategic and a tactical question.

How do we do it? is both a strategic and a tactical question.

Strategic questions shape the vision and destiny of your business, of which your practice is only one essential component. Tactical questions turn that vision into reality. Thus, strategic questions provide the foundation for tactical questions, just as the base provides the foundation for the middle and apex of your Planning Triangle.

First ask: What do we do and how do we do it . . . *strategically?*

And then: What do we do and how do we do it . . . *practically?*

Let's look at how the three plans will help you develop your practice.

The Business Plan

Your business plan will determine what you choose to do in your optometry practice and the way you choose to do it. Without a business plan, your practice can do little more than survive. And even that will take more than a little luck.

Without a business plan, you're treading water in a deep pool with no shore in sight. You're working against the natural flow.

I'm not talking about the traditional business plan that is taught in business schools. No, this business plan reads like a story—the most important story you will ever tell.

Your business plan must clearly describe:

- The business you are creating
- The purpose it will serve
- The vision it will pursue
- The process through which you will turn that vision into a reality
- The way money will be used to realize your vision

Build your business plan with *business* language, not *practice* language (the language of the optometrist). Make sure the plan focuses on matters of interest to your lenders and shareholders rather than just your technicians. It should rely on demographics and psychographics to tell you who buys and why; it should also include projections for return on investment and return on equity. Use it to detail both the market and the strategy through which you intend to become a leader in that market, not as an optometrist but as a business enterprise.

The business plan, though absolutely essential, is only one of three critical plans every optometrist needs to create and implement. Now let's take a look at the practice plan.

The Practice Plan

The practice plan includes everything an optometrist needs to know, have, and do in order to deliver his or her promise to a patient on time, every time.

Every task should prompt you to ask three questions:

1. What do I need to know?
2. What do I need to have?
3. What do I need to do?

What Do I Need to *Know?*

What information do I need to satisfy my promise on time, every time, exactly as promised? In order to recognize what you need to know, you must understand the expectations and limitations of others, including your patients, administrators, opticians, and other employees. Are you clear on those expectations? Don't make the mistake of assuming you know. Instead, create a need-to-know checklist to make sure you ask all the necessary questions.

A need-to-know checklist might look like this:

- What are the expectations of my patients?
- What are the expectations of my associate ODs?

- What are the expectations of my staff?
- What are the expectations of my vendors?

What Do I Need to *Have?*

This question raises the issue of resources—namely, money, people, and time. If you don't have enough money to finance operations, how can you fulfill those expectations without creating cash-flow problems? If you don't have enough trained people, what happens then? And if you don't have enough time to manage your practice, what happens when you can't be in two places at once?

Don't assume that you can get what you need when you need it. Most often, you can't. And even if you can get what you need at the last minute, you'll pay dearly for it.

What Do I Need to *Do?*

The focus here is on actions to be started and finished. What do I need to do to fulfill the expectations of this patient on time, every time, exactly as promised? For example, what exactly are the steps to perform when seeing someone with glaucoma, or when fitting a patient for multifocal contact lenses?

Your patients fall into distinct categories, and those categories make up your practice. The best optometry practices will invariably focus on fewer and fewer categories as they discover the importance of doing one thing better than anyone else.

Answering the question *What do I need to do?* demands a series of action plans, including:

- The objective to be achieved
- The standards by which you will know that the objective has been achieved
- The benchmarks you need to read or reach in order for the objective to be achieved

- The function/person accountable for the completion of the benchmarks
- The budget for the completion of each benchmark
- The time by which each benchmark must be completed

Your action plans should become the foundation for the completion plans. And the reason you need completion plans is to ensure that everything you do is not only realistic but can also be managed.

The Completion Plan

If the practice plan gives you results and provides you with standards, the completion plan tells you everything you need to know about every benchmark in the practice plan—that is, how you're going to fulfill patient expectations on time, every time, as promised. In other words, how you're going to arrange a refractive surgery, issue a prescription for new lenses, or educate a patient about her astigmatism.

The completion plan is essentially the operations manual, providing information about the details of doing tactical work. It is a guide to tell the people responsible for doing that work exactly how to do it.

Every completion plan becomes a part of the knowledge base of your business. No completion plan goes to waste. Every completion plan becomes a kind of textbook that explains to new employees or new associates joining your team how your practice operates in a way that distinguishes it from all other optometry practices.

To return to an earlier example, the completion plan for making a Big Mac is explicitly described in the *McDonald's Operation Manual*, as is every completion plan needed to run a McDonald's business.

The completion plan for an optometrist might include the step-by-step details of how to map out a patient's cornea using a corneal topographer—in contrast to how everyone else has learned to do it. Of course, all those who work in optometry have used a corneal topographer. They've learned to do it the same way everyone else has learned to do it. But if you are going to stand out as unique in the minds of your patients, employees, and others, you must invent your own way of doing even ordinary things.

Perhaps you'll decide that a mandatory part of your corneal topographic procedure is to print the completed map and show it to the patient, explaining what the different colors and numbers mean so that she has a better understanding of her own vision. If no other optometrist your patient has seen has ever taken the time to explain the procedure, you'll immediately set yourself apart. You must constantly raise the questions: *How do we do it here? How should we do it here?*

The quality of your answers will determine how effectively you distinguish your practice from every other optometrist's practice.

Benchmarks

You can measure the movement of your practice—from what it is today to what it will be in the future—using business benchmarks. These are the goals you want your business to achieve during its lifetime.

Your benchmarks should include the following:

- Financial benchmarks
- Emotional benchmarks (the impact your practice will have on everyone who comes into contact with it)
- Performance benchmarks
- Patient benchmarks (Who are they? Why do they come to you? What will your practice give them that no one else will?)
- Employee benchmarks (How do you grow people? How do you find people who want to grow? How do you create a school in your practice that will teach your people skills they can't learn anywhere else?)

Your business benchmarks will reflect (1) the position your practice will hold in the minds and hearts of your patients, employees, and investors, and (2) how you intend to make that position a reality through the systems you develop.

Your benchmarks will describe how your management team will take shape and what systems you will need to develop so that your managers, just like McDonald's managers, will be able to produce the results for which they will be held accountable.

Benefits of the Planning Triangle

By implementing the Planning Triangle, you will discover:

- What your practice will look, act, and feel like when it's fully evolved
- When that's going to happen
- How much money you will make

And much, much more.

These, then, are the primary purposes of the three critical plans: (1) to clarify precisely what needs to be done to get what the optometrist wants from his or her practice and life, and (2) to define the specific steps by which it will happen.

First *this* must happen, then *that* must happen. One, two, three. By monitoring your progress, step by step, you can determine whether you're on the right track.

That's what planning is all about. It's about creating a standard—a yardstick—against which you will be able to measure your performance.

Failing to create such a standard is like throwing a straw into a hurricane. Who knows where that straw will land?

Have you taken the leap? Have you accepted that the word *business* and the word *practice* are not synonymous? That a practice relies on the optometrist and a business relies on other people plus a system?

Because most optometrists are control freaks, 99 percent of today's optometry companies are practices, not businesses.

The result, as a friend of mine says, is that "optometrists are spending all day stamping out fires when all around them the forest is ablaze. They're out of touch, and that optometrist better take control of the practice before someone else does."

Because optometrists are never taught to think like businesspeople, the medical professional is forever at war with the businessperson. This is especially evident in large eye care companies, where bureaucrats (businesspeople) often try to control optometrists (medical professionals). They usually end up treating each other as combatants. In fact, the single greatest reason optometrists become entrepreneurs is to divorce such bureaucrats and to begin to reinvent the optometric enterprise.

That's you. Now the divorce is over and a new love affair has begun. You're an optometrist with a plan! Who wouldn't want to do business with such a person?

Now let's take the next step in our strategic odyssey and take a closer look at the subject of *management*. But before we do, let's listen to what Riley has to say on the subject of planning. ✤

> To find out exactly what your three critical plans will look like when they're finished, go to www.michaelegerber.com/co-author.

CHAPTER 6

Planning Your Course

Riley F. Uglum

You can't overestimate the need to plan and prepare. In most of the mistakes I've made, there has been this common theme of inadequate planning beforehand. You really can't overprepare in business!

—Chris Corrigan

I always thought I was planning. I planned to make more money next year. I planned to make my patients happy and to keep my staff motivated. I planned on taking more time off and becoming less stressed next year. I planned on selling my practice for a nice profit at some point and living happily ever after.

But it's pretty obvious now that I wasn't really planning—I was just wishing and hoping. But hey now, it wasn't really my fault, was it? I mean, I was so busy taking care of patients and doing administrative stuff that there was no time for serious planning. Without me in the exam rooms taking care of patients, there would be no practice at all. It all depended on my doctor skills. I was successful enough to be busy, and the busyness just consumed all the time and energy I had.

After the patients were gone and the doors locked, there were charts to finish, interpretation and reports to document, letters to dictate, staff e-mails to answer, and calls to return. The nonclinic days were most often devoted to HR work, staff support, staff training, staff scheduling, financial management, marketing strategies, customer service issues, lab troubleshooting, facility maintenance, IT issues, equipment upgrades, equipment service agreements, equipment maintenance, optical inventory, optical management, continuing-education planning and attendance, staff turnover, staff recruitment, staff interrelationship problems, implementing new practice management strategies, and dealing with various other management issues that presented themselves in a typical week. And of course, there were always the emergency "red eye" or eye injury visits that always occurred at inopportune times. I'm getting tired just writing about all of this stuff!

The "overwhelm" I experienced during this period often made me wonder what would have happened had I picked a different career. Would I still find myself waking up in the middle of the night wondering how I could make it through another week of this crap? What would it be like to just punch the clock at the end of the day and walk away from the job?

No, I wouldn't want to do that because then I wouldn't be able to call myself an entrepreneur, would I? And I wouldn't be able to take time off when I wanted and be in control of my own destiny. Ha! As if I were exerting any kind of control over my destiny. Sure, I could take time off if I wished, but the overhead and staff costs kept right on going, and there was always hell to pay catching up when I got back.

Getting Out of Tactical Mode

So you can see that I had good reasons for not being able to do the serious planning stuff. But I always figured, *or hoped*, that there was a better, more efficient, and more satisfying way to practice optometry waiting for me out there. And maybe if I could just read enough management journals, attend enough practice management seminars and hire the right consultants, I could find "The Way." What I found instead was that traditional practice management channels were teaching me to do what E-Myth refers to as tactical stuff, such as:

- Delegating more duties to staff
- Seeing more patients in less time
- Pre-appointing
- Internally marketing to my patients
- Asking for referrals
- Learning new clinical skills and properly billing for them
- Making my optical more profitable
- Managing and training staff
- Using technology to provide better care and perception to my patients

These techniques are effective in growing a practice on a tactical level, but once a practice becomes busy, a strategic plan is needed. Operating on the tactical level is what I refer to as "being in the trenches." Soldiers in the trenches do tactical and technical stuff like firing weapons at the enemy. Generals are well-removed from the action and do the strategic planning. If a general is in the trenches, there is no way he can see the whole battlefield and create the plan needed to win the battle or the war.

In the business world, generals are referred to as CEOs. The problem with private practice optometrists and other health care professionals is that they get so consumed with their "in the trenches" mentality that they never learn any strategic CEO planning skills. I know because I was there and didn't yet realize that the way out was to have a plan.

My practice was good at a lot of tactical things. I was a good clinician, I had great, high-tech equipment, I had great staff, and we did all of this in a great facility. But I had no overall strategic plan for all of these tactics to fit into. I was fighting and winning my tactical battles each day with no idea whatsoever what the war was about. I had no idea what my primary aim in life was, nor what my unique abilities might be as an entrepreneur. I was just an employee technician, totally consumed with performing the tactical "stuff" in my practice.

Getting into Strategic Mode—Planning Instead of Doing

E-Myth Mastery taught me to begin thinking from a strategic CEO-type perspective, and I was able to formulate the plan I needed to begin reducing my "trench time." It's really all about separation: separating myself from the business and looking at it as a separate entity. But my initial reaction to this approach was impatience. I was looking for a quick tactical-type fix because that's just the way my mind was accustomed to working. And it's a bit scary breaking out of an old mindset, even when that mentality is creating all of your business frustrations.

I'm not going to reiterate Michael's great work on the Planning Triangle. I'll just tell you how it worked for me as I went through E-Myth Mastery. And it all started with discovering my primary aim. We are all hard-wired with certain strengths and weaknesses, and life tends to be more enjoyable when we are able to do the things we are really good at. Our primary aim is all about discovering what we love to do and then building a business that allows us to take advantage of it.

This tends to be a difficult exercise for most people because we have been trained from a young age to always work on our weakness. If our report cards had mostly A's and B's with one D, we were instructed to work on improving our skills in that D area, weren't we? We got the good grades in the subjects that we enjoyed but were forced to work harder in the areas that we hated. So we spent time attempting to improve skills for which we had no innate ability or affinity. At best, we would become slightly above average in performing them. The real tragedy was that we weren't able to hone and fine-tune the skills we were naturally good at, nor could we enjoy the whole process.

Identifying Our Strengths and Using Them Strategically

All successful entrepreneurs understand that success depends on doing what you are good at and what you love (your primary aim). Everything else needs to be delegated. You will find that the world is an interesting mix of skill sets. There are a multitude of people out there who love to do the things you hate and vice versa. The best business team is composed of individuals who are good at different things but have all the bases covered collectively. Imagine going to work in a business where everyone gets to do the things that he or she loves and is good at. Or look at the other side of the coin and imagine hiring for a front desk position simply because an applicant had experience in another eye care practice. If that person were a great frame stylist in the other business, he or she may not enjoy nor be very competent at answering phones, making appointments, and dealing with the other front desk duties all day.

So how do we determine our strengths or how a prospective staff recruit might fit into our business structure? There are various tools available, but we like to use the Kolbe A profile. It helps us create balance in our team by ensuring that we cover for each other's weaknesses while ensuring that staff members not only do what they are good at but also what they enjoy. Each position at Eye Care Associates has an ideal Kolbe profile, and we use this as a filter during the hiring process. The profile is also one of the first things we want to know about our new clients at Promethean Ventures, as it helps us to coach their strengths and delegate their weaknesses to staff.

Once I found my primary aim, it helped me create the strategic objectives that form the base of Michael's triangle, or the business plan. And along with those objectives, strategic indicators were created to measure my progress. So, armed with a strategic business plan, I began the process of transforming my practice into a business.

Asking Questions

We know by E-Myth definition that a business cannot be dependent on one person for its existence. One of the practice plan questions I asked here was, "What do I need for this to happen?" The answer was obviously another doctor. So additional questions were then asked, such as:

- What gross production would a two-doctor business need to sustain the owner and the associate?
- How would a portion of the equity be sold to a prospective co-owner?
- What kind of marketing plan for new services would the new business need?
- What kind of recruiting system would the business need to attract high-quality doctors?
- What kind of compensation system will be used?
- How will patient and staff scheduling systems be affected?
- How will the new doctor's skills and effectiveness be evaluated?

And on and on and on till all the questions have been asked.

Some of the questions are strategic (business plan) questions, some are a combination of strategic and tactical (practice plan), and some are primarily tactical (completion plan). The business plan told me where I wanted to go (the vision or big picture), the practice plan told me what assets (people, facility, equipment, money) I needed to get there, and the completion plan told me what systems were necessary to ensure those assets were utilized properly.

The end result is that I can now replicate the experience I give my patients through another doctor. More patients are receiving great care, and another doctor is experiencing the joy involved with being part of a truly vibrant business. Our staff members enjoy being employed by a business that helps them get more out of life by way of the unique chemistry that the business provides them. And we are strategically planning ways to not only survive, but to thrive in the uncertain health care climate we will face in the very near future.

Wow! I'm no longer just showing up for a job and wondering how I'm going to make it through the day. E-Myth planning strategies adapted to an optometric business environment have shown me how to break out of that trap. Strategically, we know where we want to go. Assets and tactics are continually being refined to help us get there. Systems have been developed for almost everything we do in the business, along with the standards, benchmarks, and accountabilities necessary to properly execute those systems. New systems are created as needed to move us toward our strategic benchmarks. Old systems are continually innovated for the same reason.

Finding the Time and Resources to Plan

I know what you're thinking right now. "This planning stuff sounds great, but I just don't have the time to do it." Trust me. I was thinking exactly the same thing not long ago. And I'm living proof that it can be done. Here is how I did it and how we teach it at Promethean Ventures:

Leverage people by delegating all but those things that a doctor needs to do. This not only includes your staff but other outsourcing channels such as virtual assistants, videos, web-based resources, technology, equipment, and facility.

Develop solid financial skills that enable you to more comfortably transform your practice into a business. The biggest fears in making this transition are usually the financial implications involved with hiring more staff, recruiting a new doctor, or purchasing the equipment that allows you to delegate.

Don't reinvent the wheel. I've done this and stubbed my toes many times. Learn from those who already possess the wisdom.

Keep an open mind. Many of the things I now do required a paradigm shift out of an old mindset. Remember that you don't know what you don't know. Also remember that prosperous individuals do things differently than most other people. Planning is one of those things! ✤

CHAPTER 7

On the Subject of Management

Michael E. Gerber

Good management consists of showing average people how to do the
work of superior people.

—John D. Rockefeller

Every optometrist, including Steve, eventually faces the issues of management. Most face it badly.

Why do so many optometrists suffer from a kind of paralysis when it comes to dealing with management? Why are so few able to get their optometry practice to work the way they want it to and to run it on time? Why are their managers (if they have any) seemingly so inept?

There are two main problems. First, the optometrist usually abdicates accountability for management by hiring an office manager. Thus, the optometrist is working hand in glove with someone who is supposed to do the managing. But the optometrist is unmanageable himself!

The optometrist doesn't think like a manager because he doesn't think he is a manager. He's an optometrist! He rules the roost. And so he gets the office manager to take care of stuff like scheduling appointments, keeping his calendar, collecting receivables, hiring/firing, and much more.

Second, no matter who does the managing, they usually have a completely dysfunctional idea of what it means to manage. They're trying to manage people, contrary to what is needed.

We often hear that a good manager must be a "people person." Someone who loves to nourish, figure out, support, care for, teach, baby, monitor, mentor, direct, track, motivate, and, if all else fails, threaten or beat up her people.

Don't believe it. Management has far less to do with people than you've been led to believe.

In fact, despite the claims of every management book written by management gurus (who have seldom managed anything), no one—with the exception of a few bloodthirsty tyrants—has ever learned how to manage people.

And the reason is simple: People are almost impossible to manage.

Yes, it's true. People are unmanageable. They're inconsistent, unpredictable, unchangeable, unrepentant, irrepressible, and generally impossible.

Doesn't knowing this make you feel better? Now you understand why you've had all those problems! Do you feel the relief, the heavy stone lifted from your chest?

The time has come to fully understand what management is really all about. Rather than managing *people*, management is really all about managing a *process*, a step-by-step way of doing things, which, combined with other processes, becomes a system. For example:

- The process for on-time scheduling
- The process for answering the telephone
- The process for greeting a patient
- The process for organizing patient files

Thus, a process is the step-by-step way of doing something over time. Considered as a whole, these processes are a system:

- The on-time scheduling system
- The telephone answering system
- The patient greeting system
- The file organization system

Instead of managing people, then, the truly effective manager has been taught a system for managing a process through which people get things done.

More precisely, managers and their people, *together*, manage the processes—the systems—that comprise your business. Management is less about *who* get things done in your business than about *how* things get done.

In fact, great managers are not fascinated with people, but with how things get done through people. Great managers are masters at figuring out how to get things done effectively and efficiently through people using extraordinary systems.

Great managers constantly ask key questions:

- What is the result we intend to produce?
- Are we producing that result every single time?
- If we're not producing that result every single time, why not?
- If we are producing that result every single time, how could we produce even better results?
- Do we lack a system? If so, what would that system look like if we were to create it?
- If we have a system, why aren't we using it?

And so forth.

In short, a great manager can leave the office fully assured that it will run at least as well as it does when he or she is physically in the room.

Great managers are those who use a great management system. A system that shouts, "This is *how* we manage here." Not, "This is *who* manages here."

In a truly effective company, how you manage is always more important than who manages. Provided a system is in place, how you manage is transferable, whereas who manages isn't. *How* you manage can be taught, whereas *who* manages can't be.

When a company is dependent on *who* manages—Katie, Kim, or Kevin—that business is in serious jeopardy. Because when Katie, Kim, or Kevin leaves, that business has to start over again. What an enormous waste of time and resources!

Even worse, when a company is dependent on *who* manages, you can bet all the managers in that business are doing their own thing. What could be more unproductive than ten managers who each manage in a unique way? How in the world could you possibly manage those managers?

The answer is: You can't. Because it takes you right back to trying to manage *people* again.

And, as I hope you now know, that's impossible.

In this chapter, I often refer to managers in the plural. I know that most optometrists only have one manager—the office manager. And so you may be thinking that a management system isn't so important in a small optometry practice. After all, the office manager does whatever an office manager does (and thank God because you don't want to do it).

But if your practice is ever going to turn into the business it could become, and if that business is ever going to turn into the enterprise of your dreams, then the questions you ask about how the office manager manages your affairs are critical ones. Because until you come to grips with your dual role as owner and key employee, and the relationship your manager has to those two roles, your practice/business/enterprise will never realize its potential. Thus the need for a management system.

Management System

What, then, is a management system?

The E-Myth says that a management system is the method by which every manager innovates, quantifies, orchestrates, and then monitors the systems through which your practice produces the results you expect.

According to the E-Myth, a manager's job is simple:

A manager's job is to invent the systems through which the owner's vision is consistently and faithfully manifested at the operating level of the business.

Which brings us right back to the purpose of your business and the need for an entrepreneurial vision.

Are you beginning to see what I'm trying to share with you? That your business is one single thing? And that all the subjects we're discussing here—money, planning, management, and so on—are all about doing one thing well?

That one thing is the one thing your practice is intended to do: distinguish your optometry business from all others.

It is the manager's role to make certain it all fits. And it's your role as entrepreneur to make sure your manager knows what the business is supposed to look, act, and feel like when it's finally done. As clearly as you know how, you must convey to your manager what you know to be true—your vision, your picture of the business when it's finally done. In this way, your vision is translated into your manager's marching orders every day he or she reports to work.

Unless that vision is embraced by your manager, you and your people will suffer from the tyranny of routine. And your business will suffer from it, too.

Now let's move on to *people*. Because, as we know, it's people who are causing all our problems. But first let's see how E-Myth management insights affected Riley's optometry business. ❧

Managing the Unmanageable

Riley F. Uglum

*So much of what we call management consists in making it difficult for
people to work.*

—Peter F. Drucker

I thought I had arrived as an optometrist when I got to the point
that I needed an office manager. I was too busy seeing patients
to deal with management issues anymore, and I could now
afford to hire someone else to do this for me. But for some reason,
I still felt like I was spending too much time on management stuff.
And I was. Although the manager took some of the burden away,
she still needed to get my approval on almost everything she did.
Things like:

- Private accounts receivables are increasing—what do you
  think about modifying credit policy?
- The staff would like the day after Christmas off—what do
  you think?

- This equipment service agreement increased 10 percent— should I pay it?

- Three staff have asked for time off at the same time—should I grant it?

- Optical wants to take on a new frame line—what should I tell them?

As the questions became more numerous and more time-consuming to answer, I began to just let the office manager start making these decisions on her own. After all, isn't that the reason she was hired? I'm too busy seeing patients to deal with all this stuff. And this goes pretty well for a while.

But then, the office manager makes a bad decision, just as I might have done myself. However, when that decision is different than the one I would have made under similar circumstances, and something goes wrong as a result of that decision, a different dynamic is created. And it has the potential to create bad chemistry in the owner-manager relationship. I know this, because my wife, Kathy, was my first office manager.

It's not that the office manager has bad intentions, because Kathy certainly didn't. And she's a smart, business-savvy person, so it wasn't an intellect problem, either. It's just that as she became more comfortable making decisions on her own, she also put her subjective slant on things. And this slant was sometimes different from mine. We both knew that we wanted the business to grow and be successful. We just weren't on the same wavelength all the time as to how this growth and success should be managed.

This is exactly how most small businesses are operated. They hire smart and capable managers, and then rely on their instincts to manage other people in the best interests of the business. But it seldom works because people are so unpredictable, both managers and managees. Kathy and I had been married for a long time when we went through this phase. We knew each other quite well, but still couldn't get it right. We were each doing our own thing.

The Owner's Vision Lives in the Systems

What finally brought us together was the realization that we needed to be managing a process instead of managing people. We needed systems that supported our strategic objectives. We needed a business controlled by systems that were created from the owner's vision, instead of a manager using his or her own set of values.

So, in the case of the aforementioned situations, the manager should have referred to:

- The private-pay accounts receivables (AR) system
- The holiday staffing system
- The equipment service agreement system
- The minimum staffing system
- The optical frame inventory system

And if a situation arises for which there is no system, or for which the existing system isn't adequate, then a new system should be created, or an existing one innovated, while keeping the owner's vision for the business "top of mind."

The obvious thing here is that if the owner has not created a vision for the business in the first place, the manager will have no idea what type of systems to create. Because it is that entrepreneurial vision (created by a strategic planning process) that determines what management systems are needed and how those systems are designed.

By way of example, let's look at how a strategic vision might affect the management systems we just mentioned.

Private-pay accounts receivables system: The manager in charge of running this system would understand that the business needs positive cash flow in order to realize its strategic goals, and that system innovation would be necessary if cash flow were being compromised in the existing system. The manager would investigate possible changes to that system and bring them up at the next staff meeting for approval while reminding the rest of the staff of the owner's vision.

Holiday staffing system: The manager of this system would understand how strategically important patient perceptions are to the growth of the business and could explain to staff why it is important to be open on the day after a major holiday.

Equipment service agreement system: This manager's system would provide guidance in calculating how important this piece of equipment is in providing quality patient care and adding to the patient experience along with the cost of its downtime without a service agreement. The manager could then make an informed decision regarding the increased service agreement cost that he or she knows will be supported by the business owner.

Minimum staffing system: This system in the employee handbook guides human resources in how to handle this situation if it comes up, and the HR manager understands the minimum number of staff members necessary to provide the patient experience that the owner envisions.

Optical inventory system: The optical manager knows how this system works without looking at it because it is used so often. He or she also knows how the system supports the overall strategic objectives of the business.

So management is really based on the strategic planning done by the entrepreneurial business owner. That vision, and the owner's plan to realize it, is the bedrock upon which management systems are built. And when the staff understands that the business systems always reflect the vision, the business owner can manage the business via the systems instead of trying to manage the people themselves.

This is particularly important when it comes to replacing a staff member, either temporarily or permanently. It happens. Qualified staff members get sick, have babies, move to different locations, etc. And if those staff members take their wisdom with them when they leave (because it resides in their heads), you are in trouble.

However, if that wisdom lives in your systems, another staff member can fill in for a temporary absence by pulling out the operations manual for that position. In the event that a staff member leaves permanently, you simply use your staff recruiting system (another great system to have) to find a replacement that meets the personality profile for that position. That replacement then uses the appropriate operations manual combined with training videos customized for your office to get up to speed quickly.

Managing Innovation

Our systems are always evolving and getting better. As the health care environment changes, system innovation is a must. We do things differently than how we did five years ago, and five years from now business operations will be different from what they are today. Innovation means that we discover ways for an existing system to become more effective or efficient based on changes in the business environment. What does not change is how the systems must still support the strategic goals of the business owner.

Organizational Charts

E-Myth taught me how to use organizational charts to facilitate the management process. This is particularly valuable for those doctors whose spouse is involved in the practice, as Kathy was in mine. As systems are developed and innovated, your staff will occasionally have questions about how a given system should operate. Before having an organizational chart, there was always confusion over whether staff members should ask Kathy, me, or their immediate supervisor. In many cases they would ask all of us and get three different answers. This created tension and conflict, both of which are undesirable and can be avoided by using an org chart.

An organizational chart may seem ridiculous in a small health care business environment, but it's not. Remember that it's not about where your practice is now, but rather what your business will look like in the future. It needs to reflect your strategic vision, which should be to build a business that isn't dependent on you. Granted, your initial org chart may have your name in many of the boxes. But as you move closer to your strategic objectives, more staff will be hired and those boxes will be filled by other people, who then manage the systems contained in that box. And it just so happens that people are what Michael and I will discuss next. So let's move on. ✤

On the Subject of People

Michael E. Gerber

Very few people go to the doctor when they have a cold.
They go to the theatre instead.

—Oscar Wilde

Every optometrist I've ever met has complained about people. About employees: "They come in late, they go home early, they have the focus of an antique camera!"

About insurance companies: "They're living in a nonparallel universe!"

About patients: "They want me to repair forty years of bad habits and inadequate eye care!"

People, people, people. Every optometrist's nemesis. And at the heart of it all are the people who work for you.

"By the time I tell them how to do it, I could have done it twenty times myself!" "How come nobody listens to what I say?" "Why is it nobody ever does what I ask them to do?" Does this sound like you?

So what's the problem with people? To answer that, think back to the last time you walked into an optometrist's office. What did you see in the people's faces?

Most people working in optometry are harried. You can see it in their expressions. They're negative. They're tired. They're humorless. And with good reason! After all, they're surrounded by people who have headaches, eye diseases, poor vision, poor health, or—worst-case scenario—may even be going blind. Patients are looking for nurturing, for empathy, for care. And many are either terrified or depressed. They don't want to be there.

Is it any wonder employees at most optometry practices are disgruntled? They're surrounded by unhappy people all day. They're answering the same questions 24/7. And most of the time, the optometrist has no time for them. He or she is too busy leading a dysfunctional life.

Working with people brings great joy—and monumental frustration. And so it is with optometrists and their people. But why? And what can we do about it?

Let's look at the typical optometrist—who this person is and isn't.

Most optometrists are unprepared to use other people to get results. Not because they can't find people, but because they are fixated on getting the results themselves. In other words, most optometrists are not the businesspeople they need to be, but *technicians suffering from an entrepreneurial seizure.*

Am I talking about you? What were you doing before you became an entrepreneur?

Were you an associate optometrist working at a large public organization? A midsized optical company? A small eye clinic?

Didn't you imagine owning your own practice as the way out?

Didn't you think that because you knew how to do the technical work—because you knew so much about geriatric or ophthalmology or vision therapy—that you were automatically prepared to create a practice that does that type of work?

Didn't you figure that by creating your own practice you could dump the boss once and for all? How else to get rid of that impossible person, the one driving you crazy, the one who never let you do your own thing, the one who was the main reason you decided to take the leap into a business of your own in the first place?

Didn't you start your own practice so that you could become your own boss?

And didn't you imagine that once you became your own boss, you would be free to do whatever you wanted to do—and to take home *all* the money?

Honestly, isn't that what you imagined? So you went into business for yourself and immediately dived into work.

Doing it, doing it, doing it.

Busy, busy, busy.

Until one day you realized (or maybe not) that you were doing all of the work. You were doing everything you knew how to do, plus a lot more you knew nothing about. Building sweat equity, you thought.

In reality, a technician suffering from an entrepreneurial seizure.

You were just hoping to make a buck in your own practice. And sometimes you did earn a wage. But other times you didn't. You were the one signing the checks, all right, but they went to other people.

Does this sound familiar? Is it driving you crazy?

Well, relax, because we're going to show you the right way to do it this time.

Read carefully. Be mindful of the moment. You are about to learn the secret you've been waiting for all your working life.

The People Law

It's critical to know this about the working life of optometrists who own their own optometry practice: *Without people, you don't own a practice, you own a job.* And it can be the worst job in the world because you're working for a lunatic! (Nothing personal—but we've got to face facts.)

Let me state what every optometrist knows: Without people, you're going to have to do it all yourself. Without human help, you're doomed to try to do too much. This isn't a breakthrough idea, but it's amazing how many optometrists ignore the truth. They end up knocking themselves out, ten to twelve hours a day. They try to do more, but less actually gets done.

The load can double you over and leave you panting. In addition to the work you're used to doing, you may also have to do the books. And the organizing. And the filing. You'll have to do the planning and the scheduling. When you own your own practice, the daily minutiae are never-ceasing—as I'm sure you've found out. Like painting the Golden Gate Bridge, it's endless. Which puts it beyond the realm of human possibility. Until you discover how to get it done by somebody else, it will continue on and on until you're a burned-out husk.

But with others helping you, things will start to drastically improve. If, that is, you truly understand how to engage people in the work you need them to do. When you learn how to do that, when you learn how to replace yourself with other people—people trained in your system—then your practice can really begin to grow. Only then will you begin to experience true freedom yourself.

What typically happens is that optometrists, knowing they need help answering the phone, filing, and so on, go out and find people who can do these things. Once they delegate these duties, however, they rarely spend any time with the hoi polloi. Deep down, they feel it's not important *how* these things get done; it's only important that they get done.

They fail to grasp the requirement for a system that makes people their greatest asset rather than their greatest liability. A system so reliable that if Chris dropped dead tomorrow, Leslie could do exactly what Chris did. That's where the People Law comes in.

The People Law says that each time you add a new person to your practice using an intelligent (turnkey) system that works, you expand your reach. And you can expand your reach almost infinitely! People allow you to be everywhere you want to be simultaneously, without actually having to be there in the flesh.

People are to an optometrist what a record was to Frank Sinatra. A Sinatra record could be (and still is) played in a million places at the same time, regardless of where Frank was. And every record sale produced royalties for Sinatra (or his estate).

With the help of other people, Sinatra created a quality recording that faithfully replicated his unique talents, then made sure it was marketed, distributed, and the revenue managed.

Your people can do the same thing for you. All *you* need to do is to create a "recording"—a system—of your unique talents, your special way of practicing optometry, and then replicate it, market it, distribute it, and manage the revenue.

Isn't that what successful businesspeople do? Make a "recording" of their most effective ways of doing business? In this way, they provide a turnkey solution to their patients' problems. A system solution that really works.

Doesn't your practice offer the same potential for you that records did for Frank Sinatra (and now for his heirs)? The ability to produce income without having to go to work every day?

Isn't that what your people could be for you? The means by which your system for practicing optometry could be faithfully replicated?

But first you've got to have a system. You have to create a unique way of doing business that you can teach to your people, that you can manage faithfully, and that you can replicate consistently, just like McDonald's.

Because without such a system, without such a "recording," without a unique way of doing business that really works, all you're left with is people doing their own thing. And that is almost always a recipe for chaos. Rather than guaranteeing consistency, it encourages mistake after mistake after mistake.

And isn't that how the problem started in the first place? People doing whatever *they* perceived they needed to do, regardless of what you wanted? People left to their own devices, with no regard for the costs of their behavior? The costs to you?

In other words, people without a system.

Can you imagine what would have happened to Frank Sinatra if he had followed that example? If every one of his recordings had been done differently? Imagine a million different versions of "My Way." It's unthinkable.

Would you buy a record like that? What if Frank was having a bad day? What if he had a sore throat?

Please hear this: The People Law is unforgiving. Without a systematic way of doing business, people are more often a liability than an asset. Unless you prepare, you'll find out too late which ones are which.

The People Law says that without a specific system for doing business; without a specific system for recruiting, hiring, and training your people to use that system; and without a specific system for managing and improving your systems, your practice will always be a crapshoot.

Do you want to roll the dice with your practice at stake? Unfortunately, that is what most optometrists are doing.

The People Law also says that you can't effectively delegate your responsibilities unless you have something specific to delegate. And that something specific is a way of doing business that works!

Frank Sinatra is gone, but his voice lives on. And someone is still counting his royalties. That's because Sinatra had a system that worked.

Do you? Let's see if Riley does, and then we will move on to the subject of *associate optometrists*. ❧

CHAPTER 10

People Needing People

Riley F. Uglum

People are definitely a company's greatest asset.
It doesn't make any difference whether the product is cars or cosmetics.
A company is only as good as the people it keeps.

—Mary Kay Ash

When I first started practicing optometry, I had no idea how important people would be in advancing my practice to ever-higher levels. I started out with one receptionist who answered the phone, made appointments, and helped with frame selection. My wife, Kathy, or I did most everything else, which included:

- Greeting patients in the waiting room
- Pre-testing them
- Refracting them
- Doing their eye health exam
- Educating them

- Screening them for contact lenses
- Doing contact lens insertion and removal training
- Frame selection
- Measuring papillary distances and seg heights
- Checking in jobs from the lab
- Dispensing new glasses
- Adjusting glasses
- Purchasing frames from company reps
- Doing basic bookkeeping
- Doing facility maintenance
- Researching new equipment purchases
- Preparing newspaper ads, phonebook ads and other basic marketing tasks
- Doing it, doing it, doing it!

I thought I was an entrepreneur. After all, I had formed a professional corporation and was in charge of my own small business. I was much better off than someone working for corporate retail. I was in control of my own destiny, right? Well, not by traditional entrepreneurial standards I wasn't.

True entrepreneurs grow their businesses consistently even in their absence. From a growth standpoint, there was no way I could have seen more than eight full exams per day if I continued doing everything myself. And I certainly could not take a week off and still expect the business to produce.

So the realization finally came that some things need to be delegated. But that meant that I needed more people. And this is just plain scary for someone who is used to doing everything himself. I imagined the horrific consequences of delegating bifocal seg height measurements to someone else. My gosh—what if it were done incorrectly? And was there really anyone out there who could measure a seg height as accurately as I could? What about patient perceptions? Wouldn't my patients perceive that the quality of their care was less if I weren't doing this measurement myself? This seems so silly now, but I remember well the fear I felt when I first considered delegating technical tasks to other people.

The Fear Factor

Fear is what holds most doctors back when it comes to using people to replicate themselves. The three primary fears for me were:

- Fear that no one else could perform their duties as well as me.
- Fear of how I would manage more people.
- Fear of the costs involved with hiring more people.

But I also feared what would happen if I didn't learn to delegate, because my choices were really very simple.

Choice 1: I could stay the way I was, which doomed me to continue doing it, doing it, doing it, and would lead to one or all of the following results:

- My practice growth curve would flatten out (which it did).
- I would burn out (got real close to doing this, too).
- I would end up with a "harvested practice" and no equity for another optometrist to purchase.

or

Choice 2: I could start to hire people and train them to do many of the technical tests that didn't require an OD degree to perform. I could clone myself, in a sense, which would allow me to be in more places at once. I could then see more patients and provide more services. This, in turn, would improve the flow of money to the practice so I could afford to hire more staff and do the whole thing again.

Action Trumps Fear

Eventually, the realities of Choice 1 became scarier (because they were reality) than the imagined fears of hiring and managing more people. *I decided to take action.* Not irrational action, but not over-analyzed action, either. There is a balance here. Some analysis is necessary, but it can also lead to paralysis.

One way around this is to not reinvent the wheel. I simply started talking to doctors who had larger staffs than mine and asked a lot of questions. Most are happy to share their wisdom and are proud of what they have accomplished. I owe a lot to those who have shared their knowledge with me over the years. I also used consultants who understood the dynamics of staff delegation. And once the action was initiated, my fears begin to subside. I began to adopt a new attitude.

I Can Do That!

I've been fortunate enough to befriend a number of prosperous people over the years, and one characteristic they all share is an attitude of "I can do that." This is just the opposite of what many people think when presented with a challenging solution to their problems or frustrations. I used to see other successful entrepreneurs leverage people effectively, but I always chose to believe that I could never do that. Notice that I use the words "chose to believe," because our beliefs most often result from choices we have made long ago. And these beliefs just run on subconscious autopilot after a while. Simply changing your belief from one of impossibility to that of "I can do that" makes an incredible difference.

So armed with this new attitude, I started slowly, adding one staff member at a time while delegating progressively more-complex technical tasks to the senior staff. Systems were an integral part of the process, especially from a training standpoint. As I developed more confidence in the process, it became much easier to do each time. Eventually, I was able to perform an eye health exam while other people were doing complex (but not doctor-critical) technical things like:

- Pre-testing
- Refracting
- Documenting the electronic medical record, or EMR (scribing)
- Performing applanation tonometry
- Doing a contact lens screening with initial lens selection and overrefraction
- Fitting multifocal and monovision contact lens patients
- Performing contact lens follow-up exams
- Preparing instruments for all medical procedures
- Handling phone-in scripts to pharmacies
- Scheduling hospital lab tests
- Educating patients on a variety of eye diseases, conditions, and therapies
- Running the optical department

And as more complex and technical tasks were delegated (and I was able to be in more places simultaneously), many good things started to happen:

- We saw more patients per day and generated more gross production.
- I was able to take more time off.
- Profits increased, which supported more staff, staff benefits, and equipment.
- We created a better experience for our patients.
- I enjoyed more one-on-one "face time" with my patients.
- My staff enjoyed the challenge, prestige, and higher income associated with performing high-level technical procedures.

The Fears Were Addressed and Conquered

Remember the three primary fears involved with people that we talked about? Let's take a look at them and see how they were handled.

1. **Fear that no one else could perform their duties as well as me.** I quickly realized that with proper training, good systems, and great technology, talented staff could learn to perform complex technical tasks very well and that patient perception was actually enhanced!

2. **Fear of how I would manage more people.** I learned that management of systems was more important than managing people. If you have good systems in place, you simply need to hire good people to run them.

3. **Fear of the costs involved with hiring more people.** Efficiencies increase dramatically when people are deployed intelligently, and these efficiencies create improvements in gross production that easily cover the increased people costs.

What Do I Delegate First?

The two questions to ask here are:

1. What delegated task will have the most effect on my bottom line?

2. What task can be most easily trained?

Conducting a visual fields test is a good example of this. It is relatively easy to train, and the fee is reimbursable at a moderate level. Plus, it frees up the doctor's time to be reimbursed at an even higher level (as all delegation does). And once trained, this technician can teach others as necessary while moving on to more complex tasks like pre-testing, scribing, or refracting.

Should Refraction Really Be Delegated?
A Game-breaker Decision!

The delegation of refraction can be a "hot button" for many ODs. They feel that it requires years of experience and that no one can do it as well as they can. I felt the same way in 1999. I was a good refractionist, I was fast, and I was confident in my results. But I was coming to hate the refractive part of the exam. I wasn't interacting with the patient in a meaningful way (which is better, one or two), and the repetitive stress was causing significant neck and shoulder pain. And if we really look at what refraction is, we realize it's simply a technical, information-gathering task.

So while attending the San Francisco Academy meetings in 1999, I purchased a fully automated refracting system. It was one of those "action trumps fear"-type decisions. I could see how technology was making it possible for a technician to refract a patient accurately. But the fears we discussed earlier were starting to surface:

- Poor results: What if the technician couldn't perform accurate refractions as well as I did? What if patients weren't happy with their new glasses? Would our remake rate go through the roof? What would patient perceptions be if I weren't doing this important test?

- Management: How would we manage more staff, the change in patient flow, equipment location, marketing, staff perceptions, and patient perceptions?

- Money: The equipment itself was expensive—$63,000 in 1999 was a lot of money. And it would require paying another staff member to operate it, along with their training costs. How would we handle the additional costs?

After these initial fear factors kicked in, the "I could never do that" feeling reared its ugly head. It told me to let this crazy idea go and move on with my more secure "doing it myself" philosophy. But I woke up in the hotel room that night with another voice asking me, "Why can't I do this? At least take the action of running a break-even analysis on this." So I got out of bed and did just that. I took an action. And I found that if I took my revenue-per-refraction metric and multiplied it by nine extra patients per week by delegating refraction (one extra exam in the morning and another in the afternoon for four and a half days), the equipment, staff training, and extra staff expense would pay for itself in less than two years. By simply addressing one of the three fears—cost—head on, I started feeling more confident.

As a result of this initial action, the equipment was purchased and my other fears were proved to be unfounded. I was actually able to see even more exams per day than my initial calculations indicated, and my remake rate *went down!* So much for the false perception that I was the greatest refractionist in the world! I was able to reduce my clinic time from four-and-a-half days per week to three while maintaining my gross production at the same level. This was a conscious lifestyle choice, as I wanted more time off at that point in my life. The other choice would have been to continue the four-and-a-half-day week, see more patients, and increase gross and net production.

One word of caution here: Delegation of refraction allows you to "crunch" your schedule significantly. So an appointment book filled only a week in advance becomes an appointment book filled only three days out. So be sure that your pre-appointing and marketing strategies have you booked consistently three weeks in advance before delegating your refractive duties.

In my case, removing myself from the refractive technician role and shifting it to other people was a great business decision. I was learning to work smarter, not harder. This is what leveraging people allowed me to do.

The Ultimate People Strategy—Moving from Practice to Business Mode

As E-Myth taught me, the practice mode of business operation requires the owner to perform his or her special technical skills within the practice in order to survive. For the practice to evolve into the business, the owner must clone these special skills into other people. In an optometry practice, this means employing other doctors. And that is the subject of the next chapter. But before we go there, let's look at one more people principle: that of instilling ownership instincts in your people.

Staff as Business Owners

My staff members are co-owners of the optometry business. This is an important principle to understand. It is obvious that every small business owner cares deeply about the success of that business. This caring is what drives them to make the business better. And this same caring drive can be instilled in the staff members who work in the business by making them owners, too.

Does this mean that they purchase stock and have a physical "piece" of the business? Not at all! For one thing, most state laws require that all shareholders in an optometry entity be optometrists. But one of the primary benefits of owning a small business is to realize some type of financial advantage. This benefit is something your staff members can identify with. They can be trained to understand that how they perform in the practice will affect their "owner's share" of that financial benefit.

My practice uses a six-month bonus system to share ownership with the staff. They receive a percentage of the net increase in business over the same six-month period for the previous year. That bonus is divided among the staff based on hours worked, seniority, and management responsibilities.

This bonus system helps our staff understand things like:

- How I treat this patient will make a difference in whether the patient returns next year and if he or she refers other patients.
- How I handle a patient complaint affects overall practice performance.

- One canceled appointment a day will dramatically affect how many dollars will be available for my bonus. I need to get it filled.

- How I present services and products to patients affects their perception of those services and products and whether they will purchase them.

- A clean, attractive facility affects patient perceptions positively.

- New equipment is necessary to provide the best care and will also affect patient perceptions in a positive way.

- Systems are necessary to ensure our patient fulfillment strategies are executed the same for each and every patient.

The staff members understand how all these details help the business grow and thrive. And they also know that when the business thrives, their bonuses are larger. Plus, a growing business is just more fun to work in. So they are now thinking like a business owner thinks. And this is a good thing! ✤

On the Subject of Associates

Michael E. Gerber

Associate yourself with men of good quality if you esteem your own reputation, for 'tis better to be alone than in bad company.

—George Washington

I f you're a sole practitioner—that is, you're selling only yourself— then your optometry company called a practice will never make the leap to an optometry company called a business. The progression from practice to business to enterprise demands that you hire other optometrists to do what you do (or don't do). Contractors call these people subcontractors; for our purposes, we'll refer to them as associate optometrists.

Contractors know that subs can be a huge problem. It's no less true for optometrists. Until you face this special business problem, your practice will never become a business, and your business will certainly never become an enterprise.

Long ago, God said, "Let there be optometrists. And so they never forget who they are in my creation, let them be damned forever to hire people exactly like themselves." Enter the associates.

Merriam-Webster's Collegiate Dictionary, Eleventh Edition, defines *sub* as "under, below, secretly; inferior to." If associate optometrists are like sub-optometrists, you could define an associate as "an inferior individual contracted to perform part or all of another's contract."

In other words, you, the optometrist, make a conscious decision to hire someone "inferior" to you to fulfill *your* commitment to *your* patient, for which you are ultimately and solely liable.

Why in the world do we do these things to ourselves? Where will this madness lead? It seems the blind are leading the blind, and the blind are paying others to do it. And when an optometrist is blind, you *know* there's a problem!

It's time to step out of the darkness and come into the light. Forget about being Mr. Nice Guy—it's time to do things that work.

Solving the Associate Optometrist Problem

Let's say you're about to hire an associate optometrist. Someone who has specific skills: pediatric, low vision, dry eye, contact lenses, whatever. It all starts with choosing the right personnel. After all, these are people to whom you are delegating your responsibility and for whose behavior you are completely liable. Do you really want to leave that choice to chance? Are you that much of a gambler? I doubt it.

If you've never worked with your new associate, how do you really know he or she is skilled? For that matter, what does "skilled" mean?

For you to make an intelligent decision about this associate optometrist, you must have a working definition of the word *skilled*. Your challenge is to know *exactly* what your expectations are, then to make sure your other optometrists operate with precisely the same expectations. Failure here almost assures a breakdown in your relationship.

I want you to write the following on a piece of paper: "By *skilled*, I mean . . ." Once you create your personal definition, it will become a standard for you and your practice, for your patients, and for your associate optometrists.

A standard, according to *Webster's Eleventh*, is something "set up and established by authority as a rule for the measure of quantity, weight, extent, value, or quality." Thus, your goal is to establish a measure of quality control, a standard of skill, which you will apply to all your associate optometrists. More important, you are also setting a standard for the performance of your company.

By creating standards for your selection of other optometrists—standards of skill, performance, integrity, financial stability, and experience—you have begun the powerful process of building a practice that can operate exactly as you expect it to.

By carefully thinking about exactly what to expect, you have already begun to improve your practice.

In this enlightened state, you will see the selection of your associates as an opportunity to define what you (1) intend to provide for your patients, (2) expect from your employees, and (3) demand for your life.

Powerful stuff, isn't it? Are you up to it? Are you ready to feel your rising power?

Don't rest on your laurels just yet. Defining those standards is only the first step you need to take. The second step is to create an *associate optometrist development system.*

An associate optometrist development system is an action plan designed to tell you what you are looking for in an associate. It includes the exact benchmarks, accountabilities, timing of fulfillment, and budget you will assign to the process of looking for associate optometrists, identifying them, recruiting them, interviewing them, training them, managing their work, auditing their performance, compensating them, reviewing them regularly, and terminating or rewarding them for their performance.

All of these things must be documented—actually *written down*—if they're going to make any difference to you, your associate optometrists, your managers, or your bank account!

And then you've got to persist with that system, come hell or high water. Just as Ray Kroc did. Just as Walt Disney did. Just as Sam Walton did.

This leads us to our next topic of discussion: the subject of *estimating*. But first we will see how Riley used an associate OD to start transitioning his optometry practice into a business. ✤

CHAPTER 12

The Associate Optometrist

Riley F. Uglum

I've been blessed to find people who are smarter than I am,
and they help me to execute the vision I have.

—Russell Simmons

"**N**o one can care for or relate to my patients as well as I can."

"There is no way another doctor can duplicate what I do in the exam room."

"I know of so many doctor partnerships that ended badly. There is no way I'm going to allow that to happen to me. I'm just going to remain a solo practitioner."

"I tried bringing in an associate but he/she just didn't care for my patients the way I did. Plus, the associate didn't work very hard and expected to have everything now that I had worked many years to achieve."

"Life is complicated enough without bringing in another doctor and all the baggage he or she will bring with them."

Have any of these thoughts ever crossed your mind? If you are a solo practitioner, or if you were one of those who were involved in a bad relationship with another doctor, I can just about guarantee that you have.

I used to entertain these thoughts quite often. I had learned the power of delegating complex technical tasks to high-quality and well-trained staff. And I built a seven-figure practice while seeing patients just three days a week. So why in the world would I go to the trouble of recruiting another doctor into the practice and risk screwing things up? Plus, an old friend fear told me that things might get worse with another doctor in the mix. And my fears were not unfounded.

A good friend and very successful OD had tried twice to bring in an associate, and in each instance things turned into a nightmare with a bad ending. He assured me he would not go through that misery again. His experience was corroborated by multiple horror stories from other classmates and ODs. All of this served to further confirm my fears. I knew there were some successful partnerships out there, but they seemed to be exceptions to the rule.

So my strategy was always to remain solo until I was ready to retire and then just sell the practice. Other ODs were selling their practices, and they weren't much older than I was. Kathy and I built a new home on a golf course, and I began playing more in preparation for retirement mode. And I began taking charge of our personal finances by studying with professional trading coaches so I could supplement our retirement income. In fact, I became proficient enough at trading to make my living that way. Then a number of things happened:

I realized that the golf and other diversions were not life-fulfilling activities for me, and that I couldn't spend my retirement doing these things every day and be truly happy.

The same thing happened with the trading; the work was not fulfilling. Everything happened on a computer screen in my home office, and there was no interaction with other human beings.

My practice revenue flattened out, which presented another set of problems:

It would be difficult to retain quality staff with no production bonuses or raises.

It would be difficult to continue purchasing new equipment that set my practice apart and provided high-quality care for my patients.

It would be difficult to sell or market a "stale" practice.

Vacations had become "guilt trips" because of the high overhead incurred with a large staff while I was gone. Vacations were very expensive!

I learned of solo-practice colleagues who couldn't work for extended periods due to sickness or injury. Disability insurance helped, but the loss of practice revenues was devastating, as was the loss of staff members who went to work elsewhere.

I discovered E-Myth, which showed me how to turn my optometry business into a satisfying and life-fulfilling experience for me, my staff, and my patients. It helped me discover my primary aim in life and how to pursue it as a true entrepreneur rather than a "mythical entrepreneur."

A Change in Perspective

These discoveries put me squarely back into the employee doctor dilemma. Except that this time it was much less a dilemma and more of an opportunity. It was the opportunity to transition the practice into a business by using people to replicate my doctor skills. And instead of focusing on the fear of what could go wrong with a new doctor, I began to look at the good things that would happen with this transition.

- I would leave my family with a systemized practice that would be sold for full value to a qualified buyer if I died or became disabled.
- My staff would still have their jobs if something happened to me.

- I would provide a wonderful opportunity for another OD to work in and eventually own a progressive, thriving private optometry practice.

- I would be able to leave the business for more than a week or two for extended vacations if I wished while it continued to support the overhead, generate profit, and increase practice equity.

- I would have more time to grow the business strategically instead of working at the tactical level all the time.

- The business would be able to add new services for my patients such as low vision, sports vision, visual training, orthokeratology, nutritional consulting, etc.

- My stagnation and burnout from the "doing it, doing it, doing it" would disappear.

Systems Rule

Of course, recruiting a new doctor all came back to systems. During E-Myth Mastery, we developed a system for staff recruitment. We identified the characteristics that were important for each position and then created ways in which to hire quality staff with these characteristics. Well, isn't an OD just another staff member in the overall scheme of the business? And couldn't I just use this same recruitment system with characteristics that the business (not practice) needed for a new OD? And couldn't I just train the OD to run the doctor systems that already existed and that we knew were successful? Of course I could. And I did.

Michael talks about "standards of skill, performance, integrity, financial stability, and experience." I thought a lot about what these standards should be for a doctor in my practice and then plugged them into our existing staff recruitment system. The same was done for the wage and benefit package. And the result provided a great systemic solution to the problem of hiring a new sub-doctor.

Once Dr. Kristy Bhend was systemically recruited and hired, she began to learn how to operate the doctor systems of the practice.

These were the tried-and-true systems that I had already developed and knew to be successful. The odds that any new doctor will be successful is greatly increased when he or she has access to high-quality systems, and I'm going to share a great example of how this works.

Systems Accelerate Profitability and Measure Performance

Kristy was able to start producing on day one because of our scribing system. She had absolutely no familiarity with how to use our electronic medical records or how we coded diagnoses or procedures. She also had no idea how we did patient education or special tests. And she had always done her own pre-testing and refraction.

So it was like landing on a different planet for her even though she had shadowed me for a couple of days before joining the practice. But my scribes took care of all record documentation and coding for her, so she was able to simply dictate her exam findings as she performed them and pay attention to patient care. Patients were then automatically escorted to appropriate special testing based on diagnosis and then to optical or contact lenses. Imagine if she had to learn a new EMR (electronic medical record) software program, coding procedures, patient education scripts, and proper patient flow on her first day. Her productivity would certainly have been much lower.

Another advantage of the scribe system was a real-time performance evaluation of Kristy. I had a trained set of eyes and ears in the exam room observing Kristy's clinical competency and her rapport with patients. And I'm happy to report that she passed with flying colors. But had she not, I would have known it much sooner because of this system.

One word of caution—before embarking on the doctor search, please be sure that you have cloned all of the technical "nondoctor" activities to qualified staff first. It makes no sense to refract when that duty can easily be delegated to staff at a much lower wage.

New doctors should be hired to perform duties that staff cannot, and with systems in place that make the transition as efficient as possible. In this way, a vibrant business evolves from an already vibrant practice. ❧

On the Subject of Estimating

Michael E. Gerber

*The way a Chihuahua goes about eating a dead elephant is to take a
bite and be very present with that bite. In spiritual growth, the definitive
act is to take one step and let tomorrow's step take care of itself.*
—William H. Houff, *Infinity in Your Hand:
A Guide for the Spiritually Curious*

One of the greatest weaknesses of optometrists is accurately
estimating how long appointments will take and then
scheduling their patients accordingly. *Webster's Collegiate
Dictionary* defines estimate as "a rough or approximate calculation."
Anyone who has visited an optometrist's waiting room knows that
those estimates can be rough indeed.

Do you want to see someone who gives you a rough approximation? What if your optometrist gave you a rough approximation of
your condition?

The fact is, we can predict many things we don't typically
predict. For example, there are ways to learn the truth about people

who come in complaining about double vision or headaches. Look at the steps of the process. Most of the things you do are standard, so develop a step-by-step system and stick to it.

In my book *The E-Myth Manager*, I raised eyebrows by suggesting that doctors eliminate the waiting room. Why? You don't need it if you're always on time. The same goes for an optometry practice. If you're always on time, then your patients don't have to wait.

What if an optometrist made this promise: on time, every time, as promised, or we pay for it.

"Impossible!" optometrists cry. "Each patient is different. We simply can't know how long each appointment will take."

Do you follow this? Since optometrists believe they're incapable of knowing how to organize their time, they build a practice based on lack of knowing and lack of control. They build a practice based on estimates.

I once had an optometrist ask me, "What happens when someone comes in for new glasses but we discover evidence of glaucoma once we do our standard testing? How can we deal with someone so unexpected? How can we give proper care and stay on schedule?"

My first thought was that it's not being dealt with now. Few optometrists are able to give generously of their time. Ask anyone who's been to an optometrist's office lately. It's chaos.

The solution is interest, attention, analysis. Try detailing what you do at the beginning of an interaction, what you do in the middle, and what you do at the end. How long does each take? In the absence of such detailed, quantified standards, everything ends up being an estimate, and a poor estimate at that.

However, a practice organized around a system has time for proper attention. It's built right into the system.

Too many optometrists have grown accustomed to thinking in terms of estimates without thinking about what the term really means. Is it any wonder many optometry practices are in trouble?

Enlightened optometrists, in contrast, banish the word *estimate* from their vocabulary. When it comes to estimating, just say no!

"But you can never be exact," optometrists have told me for years. "Close, maybe. But never exact."

I have a simple answer to that: *You have to be.* You simply can't afford to be inexact. You can't accept inexactness in yourself or in your optometry practice.

You can't go to work every day believing that your practice, the work you do, and the commitments you make are all too complex and unpredictable to be exact. With a mindset like that, you're doomed to run a sloppy ship. A ship that will eventually sink and suck you down with it!

This is so easy to avoid. Sloppiness—in both thought and action—is the root cause of your frustrations.

The solution to those frustrations is clarity. Clarity gives you the ability to set a clear direction, which fuels the momentum you need to grow your business.

Clarity, direction, momentum—they all come from insisting on exactness.

But how do you create exactness in a hopelessly inexact world? The answer is this. You discover the exactness in your practice by refusing to do any work that can't be controlled exactly.

The only other option is to analyze the market, determine where the opportunities are, and then organize your practice to be the exact provider of the services you've chosen to offer.

Two choices, and only two choices: (1) Evaluate your practice and then limit yourself to the tasks you know you can do exactly, or (2) start all over by analyzing the market, identifying the key opportunities in that market, and building a practice that operates exactly.

What you cannot do, what you must refuse to do, from this day forward, is to allow yourself to operate with an inexact mindset. It will lead you to ruin.

Which leads us inexorably back to the word I have been using through this book: *systems.*

Who makes estimates? Only optometrists who are unclear about exactly how to do the task in question. Only optometrists whose experience has taught them that if something can go wrong, it will—and to them!

I'm not suggesting that a systems solution will guarantee that you always perform exactly as promised. But I am saying that a systems solution will faithfully alert you when you're going off track, and will do it before you have to pay the price for it.

In short, with a systems solution in place, your need to estimate will be a thing of the past, both because you have organized your practice to anticipate mistakes, and because you have put into place the system to do something about those mistakes before they blow up.

There's this, too: To make a promise you intend to keep places a burden on you and your managers to dig deeply into how you intend to keep it. Such a burden will transform your intentions and increase your attention to detail.

With the promise will come dedication. With dedication will come integrity. With integrity will come consistency. With consistency will come results you can count on. And results you can count on mean that you get exactly what you hoped for at the outset of your practice: the true pride of ownership that every optometrist should experience.

This brings us to the subject of *patients*. Who are they? Why do they come to you? How can you identify yours? And who *should* your patients be? But first let's listen to what Riley has to say about estimating. It's an interesting chapter. ✤

Billing and Certainty

Riley F. Uglum

Take care of the minutes and the hours will take care of themselves.
—Lord Chesterfield

I knew this chapter was coming. And when I initially decided to write this book with Michael, I was hoping we could make the "Estimating" chapter go away. Because at that time, I really believed that running a medical model optometry clinic on time, every time was totally impossible.

And how in the world could I write about something Michael believed in and I didn't—other than to say that in this case, "Gerber is full of it. He's got a lot of great business ideas, but this isn't one of them. He's not an optometrist in the trenches. He doesn't understand how an emergency foreign-body patient or two will throw your schedule into total disarray."

Well, as it turns out, this chapter is going to get a bit weird for a lot of readers. And for others, the concepts will make perfect sense. Michael certainly understands this stuff and encouraged me to write about the process. Because it is this process from which all true entrepreneurs are born! It is what Michael's Dreaming Room is all about. It is the reason I'm writing this book, re-creating my optometry business and building a brand-new business dedicated to teaching prosperity concepts to those who so desperately need them.

So let's go back to the first paragraph for a minute and examine the third sentence, where I wrote "I really believed that . . . was totally impossible." I have come to realize that anytime I "believe" something to be true (or untrue), it usually manifests as reality in my world. It's really that simple. The process is not new. It's been around for centuries.

There have been countless books written about it, the most famous being Napoleon Hill's *Think and Grow Rich*, in which he examines the beliefs of the most successful people in modern history. So I'm not going to present a detailed explanation of its inner workings here. I'm simply going to describe how it works for me, and in particular, how it helped me deal with what Michael calls estimating.

Beliefs can be Self-limiting

We need to be very careful about what we choose to believe in. My statement in the first paragraph said that I believed it was impossible to run my clinic on time. As long as I held this negative belief, running an on-time clinic would be impossible. I would never think to investigate the possibilities of doing otherwise. Bottom line: If our beliefs are negative or self-limiting, they will prevent us from reaching our true potential as health care professionals, as entrepreneurs, and as human beings.

So this chapter that I dreaded writing is actually becoming fun, because I get to describe an important part of the process by which I'm realizing my entrepreneurial aspirations. The process is simple, yet counterintuitive precisely because of that simplicity. It requires a paradigm shift that is difficult for many to make because of their existing belief systems. But here is how it works for me. I simply take the negative belief that running my clinic on time is impossible, and turn it into a question which assumes that it is possible. That question is phrased like this: How can I run my clinic on time, every time?

Another question that was appropriate for me to ask was: How can I write a chapter in this book about running my clinic on time?

So I simply took my initial belief that something is impossible, and turned it into a question which assumes *that it is possible!* By doing so, my impossibility belief changes to one which assumes that a valid answer to the question actually exists. And as soon as the belief changes, answers begin appearing.

I told you it was simple. Deceptively so. And that's why most people don't believe it could possibly work (another impossibility belief). It's just too simple. And as long as they hold onto this impossibility belief system, they will never give themselves the chance to have the insights necessary to accomplish the seemingly impossible.

Entrepreneurial Beliefs and Questions

Entrepreneurs work this way all the time. They have the "I can do that" mentality. Seldom do they know exactly how they will do that, but they are confident that the answers will be provided to them in some way, shape, or form.

So as I write this chapter, I ask these questions over and over, especially as I'm going to sleep at night and awaken in the morning (or in the middle of the night, as is so often the case anymore). The questions are not asked with any sense of urgency, but more with a type of relaxed expectation and confidence. Because I know from experience that the answers will be provided from what Deepak Chopra calls the "ceaselessly flowing quantum soup of information and energy."

Whew! That sounds like some pretty weird stuff, doesn't it? I thought so, too, until I began to witness its effects on my life.

The answer to the second question (How can I write a chapter in this book about running my clinic on time?) came to me in less than twelve hours, and it was indeed insightful. It was simply to describe how I use this "ask myself the right question" process to create a system in my clinic that keeps us on time, every time. Cool! The chapter I dreaded writing is now going to be a blast!

The Entrepreneurial Thinking Process

So let's work through the process. Asking the question is the first step. "How can I run my clinic on time, every time?" I've learned to ignore my left-brain, analytical dialogue that usually jumps in at this point and says things like "That's impossible. That's crazy. Gerber is nuts. I'm nuts for even thinking about this. Etc., etc., etc."

I push the impossibility thinking out of my brain and just ask the question again and again while being sensitive to any information that might cross my path. Ignoring the negative thoughts is difficult at first because our beliefs about who we are, and what we are capable of, are deeply ingrained in our subconscious. There are some excellent online programs available such as Bill Harris' Centerpointe Research Institute that can help to realign your belief system.

The first thing that occurred to me when I started asking "How can I run my clinic on time, every time?" was whether doing this was really important for my business. Or was I just doing this for Michael? The answer was easy. One of the key frustrations for me, my patients, and my staff is when the clinic gets behind schedule. And it does this on a fairly regular basis. If we have any negative findings on our patient surveys, it is always about wait time. I find myself apologizing to patients multiple times on my clinic days for keeping them waiting. What a contrast it would be to run on time with no apologies being required.

I remembered this had actually happened a couple of weeks ago with an elderly patient. We had two consecutive patients "no show" late in the day, so I was able to catch up and see this lady right on schedule. I can still see her look of surprise when I walked in on time and began to visit with her. At the end of the encounter, she looked at her watch and jokingly said, "Well, I'll be able to shop for a while because my husband won't be back to pick me up for at least an hour." When I inquired as to why this was so, she replied, "I told him to and pick me up in two hours because I know you are always behind schedule at this time of the day, and I expected to be here at least that long." We joked a bit more about her extra shopping time, but I remember thinking how great it would be if we could do this for every patient.

So it was obvious that an on-time clinic system would be a valuable asset for the business. And it would definitely set us apart from the average health care practice. I wasn't just doing this for Michael.

But holy cow, my staff and I have played with countless configurations of the appointment book through the years in an attempt to stay on time. And every one of them failed in some way, shape, or form. My left brain still kept shouting that this was impossible, but I concentrated on asking my right brain "The Question" and imagining what it would be like to have a bunch of happy patients with no wait time in my clinic.

The Magic Happens

It then occurred to me that the patient's perception of "on time" is really what it is all about. Obviously, the lady described above defined her expectation as two hours and was pleasantly surprised when it was less. Exceeding that patient's expectations was a magical thing. So when thought of in this way, the end result of an on-time clinic system could be that we exceed every patient's on-time expectations. This is a totally different way of looking at the on-time system. Instead of trying to tweak the appointment book (which we already know doesn't work), let's focus on how we can affect our patients' perceptions and expectations of being on time. And this led to the next question in the process: how can we affect our patients' perceptions and expectations of being on time?

Creating a Time Warp System

Movies are generally an hour and a half long, although some last two hours or more. When you attend a movie, do you ever walk in thinking, "Man, I'm going to be sitting in this chair for the next two hours." If that were the case, you wouldn't go in the first place. No, you are anticipating an entertainment experience, and the time you sit in that seat never enters the equation—unless the movie is terrible, in which case you become uncomfortable, squirm a bit, go to the restroom, or maybe just leave the theater early.

The same thing happens at sporting events. A three-hour football game in which you trail 28-0 at halftime feels like an eternity. But a double-overtime event that you win seems timeless. Perception is everything.

So could this same time perception be controlled in my business so my patients never have the feeling of waiting? I believed it could. I also starting believing that it could be a lot of fun to create this perception for my patients, and that my staff could have fun with the process, too.

So how could we "warp" our patients' time perception in a positive way? Here are the three possibilities that came to mind for me:

Give them a pre-expectation of a length of time for their exam and then exceed that expectation.

Provide such a uniquely positive experience for them that they lose track of time during their exam (like watching a great movie or attending the exciting football game).

Reappoint special tests like optical coherence tomography, visual fields, cycloplegic exams, dry eye exams, etc., on another day, as these tests were often the "behind schedule" culprits.

My staff and I engaged in designing a system that would accomplish all of these objectives. The first was pretty simple. We used a script when we called to remind them of their appointment that educated them about the high quality of care that we provide, and that it would take two hours to provide that great care for them. We overestimated the examination time so we could then exceed their expectations.

The second objective involves engaging our patients positively from the moment they walk in the door. We utilize a "concierge staff" concept that ensures that our patients never perceive that they are waiting. Various activities are used, such as:

- iPad units that patients can use to watch an entertaining or educational video while they wait
- Inquiring about their hobbies and suggesting a suitable video on the iPad or providing an appropriate magazine article
- Nutritional consultations
- Cosmetic consultations
- Personal education on new optical products or contact lenses
- Keeping a scribe with the patient after their refraction to answer questions or explain test results until the doctor arrives
- Gift certificates to a local business or restaurant if we get held up by emergency visits
- Bringing patients a beverage of their choice, and other things that we continue to brainstorm at our staff meetings

The third piece involves reappointing to complete special tests on another day if we start running behind. We always thought it would be more inconvenient for our patients to do this (and sometimes it is if they commute thirty miles to see us, which is not uncommon). But the majority of the time, patients are a bit tired at the end of our examination process, which usually takes an hour or more. So they usually don't mind returning on another day for the other tests. And this frees up our flow so we can keep subsequent patients moving from room to room through our exam system—instead of waiting.

Sure, we still have disruptions in the schedule. But the patient's perception is so much better than with our old system.

So, by asking the question "How can I run my clinic on time, every time?" with the full expectation that there is an answer, we have been able to look at the problem in a completely different way. Thank you, Michael, for putting this chapter in the book. Without it, my patients would still be waiting. ✤

CHAPTER 15

On the Subject of Patients

Michael E. Gerber

*Some patients I see are actually draining into their bodies the diseased
thoughts of their minds.*
> —Zachary T. Bercovitz, *Wisdom for the Soul:
> Five Millennia of Prescriptions for Spiritual Healing*

When it comes to the practice of optometry, the best definition of patients I've ever heard is this:

Patients—*very special people who drive most optometrists crazy.*

Does that work for you?

After all, it's a rare patient who shows any appreciation for what
an optometrist has to go through to do the job as promised. Don't
they always think the price is too high? And don't they focus on
problems, broken promises, and the mistakes they think you make,
rather than all the ways you bend over backward to give them what
they need?

Do you ever hear other optometrists voice these complaints? More to the point, have you ever voiced them yourself? Well, you're not alone. I have yet to meet an optometrist who doesn't suffer from a strong case of patient confusion.

Patient confusion is about:

- What your patient really wants
- How to communicate effectively with your patient
- How to keep your patient truly happy
- How to deal with patient dissatisfaction
- Whom to call a patient

Confusion 1: What Does Your Patient Really Want?

Your patients aren't just people; they're very specific kinds of people. Let me share with you the six categories of patients as seen from the E-Myth marketing perspective: (1) tactile patients, (2) neutral patients, (3) withdrawal patients, (4) experimental patients, (5) transitional patients, and (6) traditional patients.

Your entire marketing strategy must be based on which type of patient you are dealing with. Each of the six patient types spends money on optometric services for very different, and identifiable, reasons. These are:

- Tactile patient get their major gratification from interacting with other people.
- Neutral patients get their major gratification from interacting with inanimate objects (computers, cars, information).
- Withdrawal patients get their major gratification from interacting with ideas (thoughts, concepts, stories).
- Experimental patients rationalize their buying decisions by perceiving that what they bought is new, revolutionary, and innovative.
- Transitional patients rationalize their buying decisions by perceiving that what they bought is dependable and reliable.

- Traditional patients rationalize their buying decisions by perceiving that what they bought is cost-effective, a good deal, and worth the money.

In short:

- If your patient is tactile, you have to emphasize the *people* of your practice.
- If your patient is neutral, you have to emphasize the *technology* of your practice.
- If your patient is a withdrawal patient, you have to emphasize the *idea* of your practice.
- If your patient is an experimental patient, you have to emphasize the *uniqueness* of your practice.
- If your patient is transitional, you have to emphasize the *dependability* of your practice.
- If your patient is traditional, you have to talk about the *financial competitiveness* of your practice.

What your patients want is determined by who they are. Who they are is regularly demonstrated by what they do. Think about the patients with whom you do business. Ask yourself: In which of the categories would I place them? What do they do for a living?

If your patient is a mechanical engineer, for example, it's probably safe to assume he's a neutral patient. If another one of your patients is a cardiologist, she's probably tactile. Accountants tend to be traditional, and software engineers are often experimental.

Having an idea about which categories your patients may fall into is very helpful to figuring out what they want. Of course, there's no exact science to it, and human beings constantly defy stereotypes. So don't take my word for it. You'll want to make your own analysis of the patients you serve.

Confusion 2: How to Communicate Effectively with Your Patient

The next step in the patient satisfaction process is to decide how to magnify the characteristics of your practice that are most likely to appeal to your preferred category of patient. That begins with what marketing people call your positioning strategy.

What do I mean by *positioning* your practice? You position your practice with words. A few well-chosen words to tell your patients exactly what they want to hear. In marketing lingo, those words are called your USP, or unique selling proposition.

For example, if you are targeting tactile patients (ones who love people), your USP could be: "Healthy Vision Eyecare, where the feelings of people *really* count!"

If you are targeting experimental patients (ones who love new, revolutionary things), your USP could be: "Healthy Vision Eyecare, where living on the edge is a way of life!" In other words, when they choose to schedule an appointment with you, they can count on both your services and equipment to be on the cutting edge of the optometric industry.

Is this starting to make sense? Do you see how the ordinary things most optometrists do to get patients can be done in a significantly more effective way?

Once you understand the essential principles of marketing the E-Myth way, the strategies by which you attract patients can make an enormous difference in your market share.

Confusion 3: How to Keep Your Patient Happy

Let's say you've overcome the first three confusions. Great. Now how do you keep your patient happy?

Very simple . . . just keep your promise! And make sure your patient *knows* you kept your promise every step of the way.

In short, giving your patients what they think they want is the key to keeping your patients (or anyone else, for that matter) really happy.

If your patients need to interact with people (high touch, tactile), make certain that they do.

If they need to interact with things (high tech, neutral), make certain that they do.

If they need to interact with ideas (in their head, withdrawal), make certain that they do.

And so forth.

At E-Myth, we call this your *patient fulfillment system*. It's the step-by-step process by which you do the task you've contracted to do and deliver what you've promised—on time, every time.

But what happens when your patients are *not* happy? What happens when you've done everything I've mentioned here and your patient is still dissatisfied?

Confusion 4: How to Deal with Patient Dissatisfaction

If you have followed each step up to this point, patient dissatisfaction will be rare. But it can and will still occur—people are people, and some people will always find a way to be dissatisfied with something. Here's what to do about it:

- Always listen to what your patients are saying. And never interrupt while they're saying it.

- After you're sure you've heard all of your patient's complaints, make absolutely certain you understand what she said by phrasing a question such as: "Can I repeat what you've just told me, Ms. Harton, to make absolutely certain I understand you?"

- Secure your patient's acknowledgment that you have heard her complaint accurately.

- Apologize for whatever your patient thinks you did that dissatisfied her … even if you didn't do it!

- After your patient has acknowledged your apology, ask her exactly what would make her happy.

- Repeat what your patient told you would make her happy, and get her acknowledgment that you have heard correctly.

- If at all possible, give your patient exactly what she has asked for.

You may be thinking, "But what if my patient wants something totally impossible?" Don't worry. If you've followed my recommendations to the letter, what your patient asks for will seldom seem unreasonable.

Confusion 5: Whom to Call a Patient

At this stage, it's important to ask yourself some questions about the kind of patients you hope to attract to your practice:

- Which types of patients would you most like to do business with?
- Where do you see your real market opportunities?
- Who would you like to work with, provide services to, and position your business for?

To what category of patient are you most drawn? A tactile patient for whom people are most important? A neutral patient for whom the mechanics of how you practice optometry is most important? An experimental patient for whom cutting-edge innovation is important? A traditional patient for whom low cost and certainty of delivery are absolutely essential?

Once you've defined your ideal patients, go after them. There's no reason you can't attract these types of people to your optometry practice and give them exactly what they want.

In short, *it's all up to you.* No mystery. No magic. Just a systematic process for shaping your practice's future. But you must have the passion to pursue the process. And you must be absolutely clear about every aspect of it.

Until you know your patients as well as you know yourself.

Until all your complaints about patients are a thing of the past.

Until you accept the undeniable fact that patient acquisition and patient satisfaction are more science than art.

But unless you're willing to grow your practice, you better not follow any of these recommendations. Because if you do what I'm suggesting, it's going to grow.

Riley will give us his insights on patients, and then we will move on to the subject of *growth.* ❧

CHAPTER 16

Your Patients Love You, Love You Not

Riley F. Uglum

Your most unhappy customers are your greatest source of learning.

—Bill Gates

E-Myth Mastery taught me all the things that Michael talks about in Chapter 15. We learned how to identify the types of patients we serve along with their needs. From that data an "ideal patient" profile was created. Our marketing systems were then designed to appeal to the needs of that ideal patient, and patient fulfillment systems were created to ensure that this patient would be thrilled with his or her experience at our office.

We actually have three ideal patient target markets, one for our clinical services, one for the retail optical side of the business, and another for contact lenses. Each profile is different demographically and psychographically. We understand what these patients want, how to communicate with them, and how to keep them happy.

Marketing Preventative Health Care to Our Patients

As an example, let's look at how our preventative health care model was created to serve a particular demographic of our patient population. Baby boomers are an attractive market segment because of their large numbers and disposable income levels. And most of them have seen their parents suffer from various diseases including cancer, dementia, stroke, and, of course, eye diseases like macular degeneration, cataract and glaucoma. They understand how their parent's poor health affected the rest of the family psychologically and financially. Nursing homes, in particular, are a source of emotional and financial strain for the families of the residents confined there. And given the choice, most baby boomers would prefer to avoid creating this problem for their families.

"Compression of morbidity" is the term used to describe how debilitating disease is avoided till the very end of our lives. It means that we stay as healthy as possible for as long as possible to not only improve the quality of our lives but the lives of our children, as well. It is a noble goal and one that appeals to the baby boomer generation on an emotional level.

Science tells us that we can now affect the aging process in three distinct ways: (1) Lifestyle changes, (2) Use of antioxidants, and (3) Increasing cellular mitochondrial production at the genetic level. By slowing down the aging process (and the diseases that go with it) we are effectively compressing our morbidity and reducing the chances of creating long-term care problems for our families.

My practice has recommended the use of antioxidant supplements for many years to slow the progression of eye disease. When we learned there was technology available to objectively measure our body's antioxidant levels, it was a no-brainer for us to implement it. So we now can effectively counsel our patients on the benefits of antioxidants in their compression-of-morbidity quest and then measure their effectiveness.

We market this concept in various ways to convey our message in a way that can be understood by each of the six categories of patients described by Michael in the previous chapter. The message is powerful and emotional when received through the proper channel.

Patient satisfaction is a simple matter in that we absolutely guarantee that they will be happy with the program and that their antioxidant scores will increase. If not, they get their money back.

Innovation Supports the USP of the Business

From a business-growth standpoint, our anti-aging program has been very successful. And we have provided great value for our patients. It also has led to the development of cosmetic anti-aging treatments for our patients' eyelids, which are non-invasive and a great alternative to Botox injections. We also employ a cutting-edge technology that increases cellular mitochondrial production by "upregulating" the genes that control this process. All these therapies are safe and backed by solid science. And they were created by innovating our original preventative health care model.

My business is positioned by the USP "Refreshingly Unique". I think you will agree at this point that we live up to that billing because of the constant innovation that takes place within it. This USP is conveyed in our marketing materials, our facility, our equipment, our staff, our attitudes, and even in how we do a new staff orientation. Let's see how that works.

A Unique Orientation for New Team Members

Before E-Myth, new team members attended their first staff meeting having no idea what was going to happen. These meetings are structured around the production metrics of the practice. The clinic, optical, and contact lens areas each have monthly production goals, and the front desk has expectations on how many patient exams need to be booked for that time period. Things like revenue per doctor hour, revenue per exam, filled slot percentage, open slot outlook, and other metrics are reviewed. I remember seeing the disillusioned looks of new employees at their first meeting. They probably were thinking: "When they recruited me here, they talked about their fantastic patient care philosophy, but now I see that they care more about the money than they do the welfare of their patients." So there was an immediate disconnect between the way we explained our patient care philosophy during recruitment and the way the business metrics of the practice were being discussed at the staff meeting.

Obviously, we didn't want new staff members thinking about our business or our patients this way. So the staff orientation system was innovated. Now when new staff members join our team, I always spend some time with them before their first staff meeting—one on one—reviewing our business philosophy and how it relates to our patients. I explain how the production metrics that we discuss at staff meetings are important in supporting our mission statement. They are shown how production dollars are allocated to maintain our facility, invest in new equipment, and compensate high-quality staff (such as themselves) to provide great care to our patients.

Once they "get it," I ask them a simple question: "Who writes your paycheck?" They usually point to me, at which point I tell them that the person who writes their paycheck is the same one who writes mine—and that is the next patient who walks in the front door!

This then leads to a conversation about doing whatever is necessary to satisfy the patient who writes that paycheck. It also leads to another question: "Who is the most important person in the practice?" The answer is: "You (the staff member) are, each and every time you interact with one of our patients."

Patient Dissatisfaction—Marketing Opportunity

With this type of training and mindset, it is seldom that we have a dissatisfied patient. We guarantee everything we do. Our patients know it, and our staff knows it. But no one is perfect, and we occasionally have patients who are not totally satisfied. Our patient surveys indicate that our problems usually stem from one of two things:

- The length of time it takes for a full exam (which is already being addressed by our new "time warp" system)
- The comfort or vision problems with new glasses or contact lenses

We address the second type of problem by looking at complaints as marketing opportunities and a chance to become a close and trusted friend to our patients. Magical things happen when we let our defenses down in front of a dissatisfied patient. Staff members are empowered to humbly do what is necessary to solve fulfillment problems. At times, the doctor needs to be involved, and if it is a day that I'm working in the business as a doctor, I handle complaints like this:

Instead of being defensive and impatient in these situations (as I used to be), and trying to save face as the "all-knowing" Dr. Uglum, I now walk into the room armed with a weird combination of humility and confidence. The first words out of my mouth are, "I'm sorry you are having a problem. What can I do to fix it?"

Then I sincerely listen to the patient's problem without interruption. Most often, the solution is a minor prescription change in a lens. Sometimes the patient wants a more comfortable frame. Occasionally it is a bit more complex, involving an eye health issue. But whatever the problem that brought the patient back with a complaint, I listen, identify, and then provide a solution. Before leaving the room, I again apologize for the inconvenience I have caused the patient and reassure that person that I will do whatever it takes to solve the problem.

We need to realize that most patients who complain have a legitimate problem, and are most often embarrassed about complaining. All we really need to do is identify their needs and satisfy them. And if it costs us a few dollars to make that happen, big deal! These dollars are the most cost-effective marketing expense we will ever incur.

Satisfied patients refer new patients, who, from an external marketing perspective, are the most expensive to attract. It is much more cost-effective (and more fun) to internally market via "word of mouth" fulfillment systems.

Unique = Magic for Your Patients and Your Business

Our patient fulfillment systems are how we de-commoditize what we do. They are how we separate ourselves from the crowd and generate patient loyalty. Most businesses look at patient complaints as negatives. So when we turn the tables and use them as opportunities for growth, they end up being a win-win-win situation. The patient wins, the business wins, and the staff wins.

Michael says there is nothing magical about this process. I agree that there is nothing special about the systems involved with patient satisfaction. But the end result is truly magical. I almost always have a warm, fuzzy moment after one of these encounters, and I like to believe my patient does, too. These types of interactions are rare in most businesses and will definitely set your practice apart from theirs. ❧

17

On the Subject of Growth

Michael E. Gerber

Growth is the only evidence of life.
—John Henry Newman, *Apologia Pro Vita Sua*

The rule of business growth says that every business, like every child, is destined to grow. Needs to grow. Is determined to grow.
Once you've created your optometry practice, once you've shaped the idea of it, the most natural thing for it to do is to . . . *grow!* And if you stop it from growing, it will die.

Once an optometrist has started a practice, it's his or her job to help it grow. To nurture it and support it in every way. To infuse it with:

- Purpose
- Passion
- Will
- Belief
- Personality
- Method

As your practice grows, it naturally changes. And as it changes from a small practice to something much bigger, you will begin to feel out of control. News flash: That's because you *are* out of control.

Your practice *has* exceeded your know-how, sprinted right past you, and now it's taunting you to keep up. That leaves you two choices: Grow as big as your practice demands you grow, or try to hold your practice at its present level—at the level you feel most comfortable.

The sad fact is that most optometrists do the latter. They try to keep their practice small, securely within their comfort zone. Doing what they know how to do, what they feel most comfortable doing. It's called playing it safe.

But as the practice grows, the number, scale, and complexity of tasks will grow, too, until they threaten to overwhelm the optometrist. More people are needed. More space. More money. Everything seems to be happening at the same time. A hundred balls are in the air at once.

As I've said throughout this book: Most optometrists are not entrepreneurs. They aren't true businesspeople at all, but technicians suffering from an entrepreneurial seizure. Their philosophy of coping with the workload can be summarized as "just do it," rather than figuring out how to get it done through other people using innovative systems to produce consistent results.

Given most optometrists' inclination to be the master juggler in their practice, it's not surprising that as complexity increases, as work expands beyond their ability to do it, as money becomes more elusive, they are just holding on, desperately juggling more and more balls. In the end, most collapse under the strain.

You can't expect your practice to stand still. You can't expect your practice to stay small. A practice that stays small and depends on you to do everything isn't a practice—it's a job!

Yes, just like your children, your business must be allowed to grow, to flourish, to change, to become more than it is. In this way, it will match your vision. And you know all about vision, right? You better. It's what you do best!

Do you feel the excitement? You should. After all, you know what your practice *is* but not what it *can be.*

It's either going to grow or die. The choice is yours, but it is a choice that must be made. If you sit back and wait for change to overtake you, you will always have to answer no to this question: Are you ready?

Riley will now relate his thoughts on growth, and then we will look at the subject of *change.* ✤

CHAPTER 18

Growing Joys

Riley F. Uglum

Without continual growth and progress, such words as improvement, achievement, and success have no meaning.

—Benjamin Franklin

I have a true story that is appropriate for this chapter on growth. New Hampton, Iowa, is home to the Davis Motorcycle Rally every September. Thousands of bikers converge on the town and fill all of the motels and campgrounds within a twenty-five-mile radius beginning on the Monday before the big weekend. Mikkelson Park is the place where all of the action takes place, and hundreds of bikers camp on the park property itself.

Directly across from the park on Highway 24 is a pizza kitchen. The next nearest restaurant is about a mile away. The current owner does more business in this one week that he does in three months serving his regular patrons. He even opens for breakfast every morning to serve the hungry bikers and wishes there were a bike rally every month.

The story here involves the previous restaurant owner, who was averse to growing his business. Before selling the business to the new owner, he chose to lock the door of his business the entire week of the bike rally. When asked why in the world he would do such a thing, his standard answer was, "Nobody needs to be that busy." Incredible! Or is it?

How many times have optometrists failed to pursue growth opportunities because it might make things more complicated? And why do they so fear this complication? It's usually because they think that they need to deal with all of the complications personally.

Why do you think the restaurant owner locked the door on the most profitable week of the year? It's because he didn't want to deal with the complications personally. He normally ran the pizza place with himself and one kitchen employee—uncomplicated. But for this event, he would have had to hire and train some temporary people, plan a breakfast meal not normally offered, order more food from his vendors, work a lot more hours, clean up the mess, etc. This was going to add some complication to his world, so he chose instead to squander this significant business growth opportunity and take the week off.

Well, I love to see my practice grow. The excitement is heady at times. I know that growth has provided many benefits for me, my staff, my patients, and my vendors. These benefits include:

- Better cash flow
- More staff support for quality patient care
- More technology support for quality patient care and delegation opportunities
- Improved patient perceptions from the higher quality of care
- Facility improvements and associated patient perceptions
- Bonuses for staff and owners
- Better vendor perceptions and support
- More jobs provided in the local economy

And the number one advantage of growth is that once you have grown enough, you can afford to delegate many of these growth complications to talented staff while you continue to pursue other growth opportunities.

Managing the Complications of Growth

If your practice is still small with limited staffing, you as an owner OD will initially need to deal with some of these growth complications. But as your growth accelerates, you will begin delegating some of the complexity to others.

I got lazy for a few years and watched my practice plateau. At the time, I thought this was okay because I was making a good living and didn't need more money. But I soon realized that adapting a no-growth philosophy was essentially the same as the restaurant owner saying, "Nobody needs to be that busy."

So really, when it comes to growth, the only logical question to ask is: How do we best manage the complications of the growth? Does the word "system" ring a bell? How about people and profit? I believe the best way to manage growth is to use the new profit generated to invest in people who will run new systems that can manage the complexity.

An example would be a practice that has implemented a new marketing system and has generated growth in the form of an appointment book that is full for two months out. The complexity is created when new patients calling for an appointment end up not scheduling because they can't wait two months to be seen.

There are multiple solutions to this problem, none of which requires the doctor to work more hours. Here are a few:

- Use new profit and anticipated profit growth to hire a new staff member and delegate pre-testing using new pre-test systems.

- Use profit to purchase automated refraction equipment and hire another staff member so that refraction can be delegated via your refraction system. This is a great way to "crunch" a schedule while still providing great care for your patients.

- Use profit to hire a scribe, which makes the exam room process much more efficient while enhancing patient perceptions.

- Once you have accomplished all of the above, it's time to recruit an associate OD with your newfound profit and have that person use your doctor systems to become efficient quickly.

This last step is actually the first step toward transforming your practice into a business. And once you begin this process, you won't look back, because you will begin to realize that this is where the fun begins. You will begin spending time on growing a business that isn't sucking the life out of you. It is now providing a meaningful way to conduct your life and supporting your primary aim.

Tracking the Growth

There are a number of metrics that help us track our growth and ensure that it is on track. I mentioned in the chapter on patients that key metrics are discussed every Tuesday at our weekly staff meeting. What I find amazing is that my staff members all know the key metrics for our business while most optometrists have no idea what theirs are. They are just too busy doing it, doing it, doing it.

As stated in the chapter on planning, we need to have strategic objectives and indicators for our business. If we understand where we want to be three years from now, we can determine what needs to happen each year, each month, each week, each day, and each hour to arrive at our goal. In my business, the basic production metrics are doctor hours and gross production per doctor hour. All significant revenue generation happens when a doctor sees patients, although there are many variables that can affect this number. So at our weekly staff meetings, the metrics are broken down like this:

- Gross production per doctor hour
- Collections as a percentage of gross production
- Refractions per doctor hour
- Revenue per refraction
- Optical production per doctor hour
- Clinic production per doctor hour
- Contact lens production per doctor hour
- Percentage of filled patient examination appointments
- Available exam appointments for next four weeks

When strategic growth goals are met or exceeded, we can see which metrics are responsible and attempt to systemize that trend. Examples might be:

- Optical was more productive due to increased second-pair sales.
- Contact lens sales improved due to newsletter promotion of multifocal contacts.
- Clinic production was up due to utilization of new diagnostic equipment.

If goals aren't being met, we can determine the etiology by using the same approach. An example would be if collections are below 95 percent of production. The reasons and solutions would be discussed (or investigated prior to the next staff meeting).

Our staff meeting metrics system is also very proactive in preventing future production lapses by using a forward-looking appointment book strategy. If there are too many open exam slots in the next ninety days, this system is employed to follow up on recalls, pre-appointments, and reactivation of inactive patients well in advance.

The other thing that happens when these metrics are shared with staff members is that they understand how they affect not only the business, but also their compensation via their bonus system. They know the effect on their six-month bonus if we see one less patient per day over that time period. And they know the cost of one dissatisfied patient versus the benefits exceeding patient expectations.

Yes, growth creates new challenges. But by utilizing money, planning, management, and people effectively, we are soon looking for other growth opportunities. And we never find ourselves saying, "Nobody needs to be that busy." ❖

CHAPTER 19

On the Subject of Change

Michael E. Gerber

There is nothing permanent except change.
—Heraclitus of Ephesus, *Lives of the Philosophers*

S o your practice is growing. That means, of course, that it's also changing. Which means it's driving you and everyone in your life crazy.

That's because, to most people, change is a diabolical thing. Tell most people they've got to change, and their first instinct is to crawl directly into a hole. Nothing threatens their existence more than change. Nothing cements their resistance more than change. Nothing!

Yet for the past thirty-five years, that's exactly what I've been proposing to small-business owners: the need to change. Not for the sake of change itself, but for the sake of their lives.

I've talked to countless optometrists whose hopes weren't being realized through their practice; whose lives were consumed by work; who slaved increasingly longer hours for decreasing pay; whose dissatisfaction grew as their enjoyment shriveled; whose practice had become the worst job in the world; whose money was out of control; whose employees were a source of never-ending hassles, just like their patients, their bank, and, increasingly, even their family.

More and more, these optometrists spent their time alone, dreading the unknown and anxious about the future. And even when they were with people, they didn't know how to relax. Their mind was always on the job. They were distracted by work, by the thought of work. By the fear of falling behind.

And yet, when confronted with their condition and offered an alternative, most of the same optometrists strenuously resisted it. They assumed that if there were a better way of doing business, they already would have figured it out. They derived comfort from knowing what they believed they already knew. They accepted the limitations of being an optometrist; or the truth about people; or the limitations of what they could expect from their patients, their employees, their associate optometrists, their bankers—even their family and friends.

In short, most optometrists I've met over the years would rather live with the frustrations they already have than risk enduring new frustrations.

Isn't that true of most people you know? Rather than opening up to the infinite number of possibilities life offers, they prefer to shut their lives down to respectable limits. After all, isn't that the most reasonable way to live?

I think not. I think we must learn to let go. I think that if you fail to embrace change, it will inevitably destroy you.

Conversely, by opening yourself to change, you give your optometry practice the opportunity to get the most from your talents.

Let me share with you an original way to think about change, about life, about who we are and what we do. About the stunning notion of expansion and contraction.

Contraction versus Expansion

"Our salvation," a wise man once said, "is to allow." That is, to be open, to let go of our beliefs, to change. Only then can we move from a point of view to a viewing point.

That wise man was Thaddeus Golas, the author of a small, powerful book entitled *The Lazy Man's Guide to Enlightenment* (Seed Center, 1971).

Among the many inspirational things he had to say was this compelling idea:

> *The basic function of each being is expanding and contracting. Expanded beings are permeative; contracted beings are dense and impermeative. Therefore each of us, alone or in combination, may appear as space, energy, or mass, depending on the ratio of expansion to contraction chosen, and what kind of vibrations each of us expresses by alternating expansion and contraction. Each being controls his or her own vibrations.*

In other words, Golas tells us that the entire mystery of life can be summed up in two words: *expansion* and *contraction*. He goes on to say:

> *We experience expansion as awareness, comprehension, understanding, or whatever we wish to call it.*
>
> *When we are completely expanded, we have a feeling of total awareness, of being one with all life.*
>
> *At that level we have no resistance to any vibrations or interactions of other beings. It is timeless bliss, with unlimited choice of consciousness, perception, and feeling.*
>
> *When a (human) being is totally contracted, he is a mass particle, completely imploded.*
>
> *To the degree that he is contracted, a being is unable to be in the same space with others, so the contraction is felt as fear, pain, unconsciousness, ignorance, hatred, evil, and a whole host of strange feelings.*
>
> *At an extreme (of contraction, a human being) has the feeling of being completely insane, of resisting everyone and everything, of being unable to choose the content of his consciousness.*
>
> *Of course, these are just the feelings appropriate to mass vibration levels, and he can get out of them at any time by expanding, by letting go of all resistance to what he thinks, sees, or feels.*

Stay with me here. Because what Golas says is profoundly important. When you're feeling oppressed, overwhelmed, exhausted by more than you can control—contracted, as Golas puts it—you can change your state to one of expansion.

According to Golas, the more contracted we are, the more threatened we are by change; the more expanded we are, the more open we are to change.

In our most enlightened—that is, open—state, change is as welcome as non-change. Everything is perceived as a part of ourselves. There is no inside or outside. Everything is one thing. Our sense of isolation is transformed to a feeling of ease, of light, of joyful relationship with everything.

As infants, we didn't even think of change in the same way, because we lived those first days in an unthreatened state. Insensitive to the threat of loss, most young children are only aware of *what is*. Change is simply another form of *what is*. Change just *is*.

However, when we are in our most contracted—that is, closed— state, change is the most extreme threat. If the known is what I have, then the unknown must be what threatens to take away what I have. Change, then, is the unknown. And the unknown is fear. It's like being between trapezes.

- To the fearful, change is threatening because things may get worse.
- To the hopeful, change is encouraging because things may get better.
- To the confident, change is inspiring because the challenge exists to improve things.

If you are fearful, you see difficulties in every opportunity. If you are fear-free, you see opportunities in every difficulty.

Fear protects what I have from being taken away. But it also disconnects me from the rest of the world. In other words, fear keeps me separate and alone.

Here's the exciting part of Golas's message: With this new understanding of contraction and expansion, we can become completely attuned to where we are at all times.

If I am afraid, suspicious, skeptical, and resistant, I am in a contracted state. If I am joyful, open, interested, and willing, I am in an expanded state. Just knowing this puts me on an expanded path. Always remembering this, Golas says, brings enlightenment, which opens me even more.

Such openness gives me the ability to freely access my options. And taking advantage of options is the best part of change. Just as there are infinite ways to greet a patient, there are infinite ways to run your practice. If you believe Thaddeus Golas, your most exciting option is to be open to all of them.

Because your life is lived on a continuum between the most contracted and most expanded—the most closed and most open—states, change is best understood as the movement from one to the other, and back again.

Most small-business owners I've met see change as a thing-in-itself, as something that just happens to them. Most experience change as a threat. Whenever change shows up at the door, they quickly slam it. Many bolt the door and pile up the furniture. Some even run for their gun.

Few of them understand that change isn't a thing-in-itself, but rather the manifestation of many things. You might call it the revelation of all possibilities. Think of it as the ability at any moment to sacrifice what we are for what we could become.

Change can either challenge us or threaten us. It's our choice. Our attitude toward change can either pave the way to success or throw up a roadblock.

Change is where opportunity lives. Without change we would stay exactly as we are. The universe would be frozen still. Time would end.

At any given moment, we are somewhere on the path between a contracted and expanded state. Most of us are in the middle of the journey, neither totally closed nor totally open. According to Golas, change is our movement from one place in the middle toward one of the two ends.

Do you want to move toward contraction or toward enlightenment? Because without change, you are hopelessly stuck with what you've got.

Without change:

- We have no hope.
- We cannot know true joy.
- We will not get better.
- We will continue to focus exclusively on what we have and the threat of losing it.

All of this negativity contracts us even more, until, at the extreme closed end of the spectrum, we become a black hole so dense that no light can escape.

Sadly, the harder we try to hold on to what we've got, the less able we are to do so. So we try still harder, which eventually drags us even deeper into the black hole of contraction.

Are you like that? Do you know anybody who is?

Think of change as the movement between where we are and where we're not. That leaves only two directions for change: either moving forward or slipping backward. We either become more contracted or more expanded.

The next step is to link change to how we feel. If we feel afraid, change is dragging us backward. If we feel open, change is pushing us forward.

Change is not a thing-in-itself, but a movement of our consciousness. By tuning in, by paying attention, we get clues to the state of our being.

Change, then, is not an outcome or something to be acquired. Change is a shift of our consciousness, of our being, of our humanity, of our attention, of our relationship with all other beings in the universe.

We are either "more in relationship" or "less in relationship." Change is the movement in either of those directions. The exciting part is that *we possess the ability to decide which way we go . . . and to know in the moment which way we're moving.*

Closed, open. . . . Open, closed. Two directions in the universe. The choice is yours.

Do you see the profound opportunity available to you? What an extraordinary way to live!

Enlightenment is not reserved for the sainted. Rather, it comes to us as we become more sensitive to ourselves. Eventually, we become our own guides, alerting ourselves to our state, moment by moment: *open ... closed ... open ... closed.*

Listen to your inner voice, your ally, and feel what it's like to be open and closed. Experience the instant of choice in both directions.

You will feel the awareness growing. It may be only a flash at first, so be alert. This feeling is accessible, but only if you avoid the black hole of contraction.

Are you afraid that you're totally contracted? Don't be—it's doubtful. The fact that you're still reading this book suggests that you're moving in the opposite direction.

You're more like a running back seeking the open field. You can see the opportunity gleaming in the distance. In the open direction.

Understand that I'm not saying that change itself is a point on the path; rather, it's the all-important movement.

Change is *in you,* not *out there.*

What path are you on? The path of liberation? Or the path of crystallization?

As we know, change can be for the better or for the worse.

If change is happening *inside* of you, it is for the worse only if you remain closed to it. The key, then, is your attitude—your acceptance or rejection of change. Change can be for the better only if you accept it. And it will certainly be for the worse if you don't.

Remember, change is nothing in itself. Without you, change doesn't exist. Change is happening inside of each of us, giving us clues to where we are at any point in time.

Rejoice in change, for it's a sign you are alive.

Are we open? Are we closed? If we're open, good things are bound to happen. If we're closed, things will only get worse.

According to Golas, it's as simple as that. Whatever happens defines where we are. *How* we are is *where* we are. It cannot be any other way.

For change is life.

Charles Darwin wrote, "It is not the strongest of the species that survive, nor the most intelligent, but the one that proves itself most responsive to change."

The growth of your optometry practice, then, is its change. Your role is to go with it, to be with it, to share the joy, embrace the opportunities, meet the challenges, learn the lessons.

Remember, there are three kinds of people: (1) those who make things happen, (2) those who let things happen, and (3) those who wonder what the hell happened. The people who make things happen are masters of change. The other two are its victims.

Which type are you?

The Big Change

If all this is going to mean anything to the life of your practice, you have to know when you're going to leave it. At what point, in your practice's rise from where it is now to where it can ultimately grow, are you going to sell it? Because if you don't have a clear picture of when you want out, your practice is the master of your destiny, not the reverse.

As we stated earlier, the most valuable form of money is equity, and unless your business vision includes your equity and how you will use it to your advantage, you will forever be consumed by your practice.

Your practice is potentially the best friend you ever had. It is your practice's nature to serve you, so let it. If, however, you are not a wise steward, if you do not tell your practice what you expect from it, it will run rampant, abuse you, use you, and confuse you.

Change. Growth. Equity.

Focus on the point in the future when you will take leave of your practice. Now reconsider your goals in that context. Be specific. Write them down.

Skipping this step is like tiptoeing through earthquake country. Who can say where the fault lies waiting? And who knows exactly when your whole world may come crashing down around you?

Which brings us to the subject of *time*. But first, let's see what Riley has to say regarding change. ❧

CHAPTER
20

The Gift of Change

Riley F. Uglum

Conformity is the jailer of freedom and the enemy of growth.
—John F. Kennedy

This chapter is dear to my heart simply because I've come to know and value change as one of my strongest allies from both a business and personal point of view. In fact, I need to be careful not to embrace change just for the sake of change, which can complicate not only my life, but the lives of my family and my staff. Fortunately for me, my wife, Kathy, provides balance in this area, and we complement each other well. But ultimately, change is what enables us to build better businesses, and even more important, better lives.

E-Myth Mastery helped me discover my primary aim, which might be described as our true calling in life. It is that which we could do every day and not consider it work. After peeling back the layers of what I thought were my primary aims, I discovered that what has always excited me the most was the process of discovery. It is my primary aim that attracted me to the sciences and ultimately to optometry. It also led me to E-Myth, and it is why I continue to look for and discover better ways to "do the optometry business" in a way that enhances all who are associated with it—including me.

But what does discovery have to do with change? It's because change was necessary in order for me to turn the discovery into a process that could improve my business. For example, I love technology and enjoy going to exhibit halls and discovering how the new equipment works. But transforming that discovery into better patient care required change. Anytime new equipment is incorporated into the practice, certain changes need to be made, such as:

- Allocating space so the equipment can be efficiently worked into our patient flow
- Training staff to use it
- Determining how I will pay for it and how rapidly I will realize a decent return on investment
- Patient education as to why patients need the test and why they should pay for it
- Managing equipment maintenance, service agreements, etc.

The alternative is stagnation. Without change, I would still be practicing in a 1,200-square-foot facility with two staff members and examining eight patients a day with outdated equipment. Michael likes to talk about expansion and contraction when he describes change. I agree. And to simplify a bit, I think that looking at the following relationships may help.

- Good relationships: Change leads to growth and evolution, which provide us with enlightenment and freedom, which in turn allow us to live life on our terms.
- Bad relationships: Lack of change leads to stagnation, contraction and fear, which create a nonenlightened existence, which then enslaves us as victims of circumstances.

These relationships are particularly applicable in the area of finance. Almost everyone who has experienced the financial pain after Sept. 11, 2001, and the collapse of the real estate markets goes into "bunker mentality mode." This is also referred to as a "lack mentality" or "poverty thinking." Optometrists pull back and stop spending money on themselves and on their practices. They also assume that everyone else is doing the same thing and that no one will spend money on eye care. The result is contraction and fear. And their fears become a self-fulfilling prophecy.

The Solution Is Change! A Change in the Way We Think!

Remember the chapter on estimating and how powerful asking positive questions can be? A cornerstone strategy of my new company, Promethean Ventures, is developing prosperity mindsets in our clients. Most of them have been instilled with "scarcity thinking" habits that are difficult to break. The media are filled with negativity, which tends to affect how they think and feel. Shifting their thoughts from scarcity to abundance involves change. But changing the way they think makes a world of difference in how they are able to positively affect their business and their lives.

I remember overhearing some of my staff members discussing the bad economy at the beginning of 2008 and knew that we needed to change that scarcity thinking. So at the next staff meeting, I simply announced that our business had decided not to participate in the recession and that they should plan on another good year for the business. They all received record bonus checks in 2009.

Tough Times = Ideal Entrepreneurial Environment

Another thing to think about as we go through tough economic times is that they are historically the best times for entrepreneurs to grow their businesses. Some of the greatest entrepreneurs of modern times started their businesses in terrible economies. That's because recessions generate needs, and if we, as strategic CEOs, can create services or products that fulfill those needs, our businesses will thrive.

And guess what the common denominator is for the creation and implementation of these services and products? Change!

Fulfilling Needs Provides True Value to Our Patients

My business recently implemented a major change in health care philosophy. We have always been good at treating unhealthy eyes, but we are now practicing preventive eye care by incorporating a more holistic model. We now have the ability to measure our patients' nutritional profile objectively and then make diet or supplementation recommendations, which most often improve their status within sixty days.

My staff and I are living proof that this nutritional system works, and our patients love it. They now understand that they can reduce their risk for rapid progression of aging-type diseases like cataracts, macular degeneration, dementia, arthritis, high blood pressure, cancer, heart disease, and the complications of diabetes. So not only is this change improving the quality of life for my patients, but it is also providing an income stream that cannot be controlled by managed care. This is all private-pay income.

The other amazing realization that has come about as a result of this change is that even in the midst of a severe recession, people feel it is important to maintain their health. Baby boomers see their parents suffering from the ravages of poor health and they don't want the same things happening to them. Nor do they want their children dealing with Mom and Dad's health problems thirty years down the road. Fulfilling needs and creating value for our patients are the keys to success regardless of how the economy is doing.

The Alternative to Changing is Higher Risk

The primary reason people resist change is the fear and uncertainty it brings to their lives. It just seems easier to do nothing than to risk doing something that might not turn out the way they thought. But they fail to realize the tremendous risk they take by doing nothing. If, for instance, private health care practices continue to assume they can maintain their profitability by accepting what managed care plans pay them, what happens when reimbursements are cut and the other costs of doing business continue to increase? This is much riskier than exploring new avenues of private-pay reimbursement as described above.

Toward the end of 2010, I received an e-mail from the Iowa Optometric Association stating that Medicare was lowering its reimbursement on Optical Coherence Tomography from $85 to $31 the following year. My business does a thousand of these tests per year. So in 2011, we are looking at a revenue decrease of more than $50,000.

Fortunately, our anti-aging subspecialty is already adding more revenue than we will lose on the tomography, and it will continue to grow in 2011. And of course the insurance companies can't control or cut this private-pay revenue stream. So by embracing change and looking at the health care environment strategically (instead of tactically), my business is now well-positioned to withstand these types of adverse events.

Technology

So many optometrists are resistant to changes in technology, even when that technology is exactly what their practice needs to grow. I understand that it can be intimidating for some. It all goes back to the fear thing, doesn't it? The simple truth here is that the health care climate is changing rapidly, and technology provides the best leverage and flexibility for adapting to that new environment.

Electronic medical records are a good example. We have used an EMR system since 1999 and still remember the anxiety we felt when we couldn't actually touch the pages in our appointment book. Or the feelings at the end of a long day when all the work we did was recorded into something we couldn't see on a paper chart. But there were significant upsides, because we then had the flexibility to access the appointment book or a patient's chart from multiple locations in the building instead of trying to chase down a piece of paper.

Just that advantage increased our efficiency many times over. One staff member could be checking diagnostic and billing codes, another could be writing an optical order, and yet another could be updating contact lens data. Plus, the doctor could be finishing up exam notes and updating the recall—all on the same patient during the same time period.

Additionally, all refractive data (lensometer, autorefractor, keratometer, topographer, aberrometer, subjective refraction) transfers into the EMR at the touch of a button with absolutely no transcription errors. Insurance claims are filed and lab orders are placed with a mouse click. At the end of the day, any staff member or doctor can pull up the day's EMRs and review them to be sure they are complete—again, from different locations and at the same time.

More and more offices are converting to EMRs now, but mostly because the medical environment is forcing it upon them. They weren't able to capitalize on the efficiencies that were available for the past ten-plus years. Instead, they are implementing old technology when more-progressive practices are looking for new technology that will allow them to further leverage their efficiency, effectiveness and *time*, which is the next topic we will explore. ❧

CHAPTER 21

On the Subject of Time

Michael E. Gerber

Take time to deliberate; but when the time for action arrives,
stop thinking and go in.

—Andrew Jackson

"I'm running out of time!" optometrists often lament. "I've got to learn how to manage my time more carefully!"

Of course, they see no real solution to this problem. They're just worrying the subject to death. Singing the optometrist's blues.

Some make a real effort to control time. Maybe they go to time management classes, or faithfully try to record their activities during every hour of the day.

But it's hopeless. Even when optometrists work harder, even when they keep precise records of their time, there's always a shortage of it. It's as if they're looking at a square clock in a round universe. Something doesn't fit. The result: The optometrist is constantly chasing work, money, life.

And the reason is simple. Optometrists don't see time for what it really is. They think of time with a small "t," rather than Time with a capital "T."

Yet Time is simply another word for *your life*. It's your ultimate asset, your gift at birth—and you can spend it any way you want. Do you know how you want to spend it? Do you have a plan?

How do *you* deal with Time? Are you even conscious of it? If you are, I bet you are constantly locked into either the future or the past. Relying on either memory or imagination.

Do you recognize these voices? "Once I get through this, I can have a drink . . . go on a vacation . . . retire." "I remember when I was young and practicing optometry was satisfying."

As you go to bed at midnight, are you thinking about waking up at 7 a.m. so that you can get to the office by 8 a.m. so that you can go to lunch by noon, because Dr. Morales will be there at 2 p.m. and you've got refractive surgery consultations scheduled for 4?

Most of us are prisoners of the future or the past. While pinballing between the two, we miss the richest moments of our life—the present. Trapped forever in memory or imagination, we are strangers to the here and now. Our future is nothing more than an extension of our past, and the present is merely the background.

It's sobering to think that right now each of us is at a precise spot somewhere between the beginning of our Time (our birth) and the end of our Time (our death).

No wonder everyone frets about Time. What really terrifies us is that *we're using up our life and we can't stop it*.

It feels as if we're plummeting toward the end with nothing to break our free fall. Time is out of control! Understandably, this is horrifying, mostly because the real issue is not time with a small "t" but Death with a big "D."

From the depths of our existential anxiety, we try to put Time in a different perspective—all the while pretending we can manage it. We talk about Time as though it were something other than what it is. "Time is money," we announce, as though that explains it.

But what every optometrist should know is that Time is life. And Time ends! Life ends!

The big, walloping, irresolvable problem is that *we don't know how much Time we have left.*

Do you feel the fear? Do you want to get over it?

Let's look at Time more seriously.

To fully grasp Time with a capital "T," you have to ask the Big Question: *How do I wish to spend the rest of my Time?*

Because I can assure you that if you don't ask that Big Question with a big "Q," you will forever be assailed by the little questions. You'll shrink the whole of your life to *this time* and *next time* and the *last time*—all the while wondering, *what time is it?*

It's like running around the deck of a sinking ship worrying about where you left the keys to your cabin.

You must accept that you have only so much Time; that you're using up that Time second by precious second. And that your Time, your life, is the most valuable asset you have. Of course, you can use your Time any way you want. But unless you choose to use it as richly, as rewardingly, as excitingly, as intelligently, as *intentionally* as possible, you'll squander it and fail to appreciate it.

Indeed, if you are oblivious to the value of your Time, you'll commit the single greatest sin: You will live your life unconscious of its passing you by.

Until you deal with Time with a capital "T," you'll worry about time with a small "t" until you have no Time—or life—left. Then your Time will be history . . . along with your life.

I can anticipate the question: If Time is the problem, why not just take on fewer patients? Well, that's certainly an option, but probably not necessary. I know an optometrist with a practice that sees three times as many patients as the average, yet he doesn't work long hours. How is it possible?

This optometrist has a system. Roughly 50 percent of what needs to be communicated to patients is "downloaded" to the opticians and office staff. By using this expert system, the employees can do everything the optometrist or his associate optometrists would do—everything that isn't optometrist-dependent.

Be versus Do

Remember when we all asked, "What do I want to be when I grow up?" It was one of our biggest concerns as children.

Notice that the question isn't, "What do I want to *do* when I grow up?" It's "What do I want to *be?*"

Shakespeare wrote, "To be or not to be." Not, "To do or not to do."

But when you grow up, people always ask you, "What do you *do?*" How did the question change from *being* to *doing?* How did we miss the critical distinction between the two?

Even as children, we sensed the distinction. The real question we were asking was not what we would end up *doing* when we grew up, but who we would *be.*

We were talking about a *life* choice, not a *work* choice. We instinctively saw it as a matter of how we spend our Time, not what we do *in* time.

Look to children for guidance. I believe that as children we instinctively saw Time as life and tried to use it wisely. As children, we wanted to make a life choice, not a work choice. As children, we didn't know—or care—that work had to be done on time, on budget.

Until you see Time for what it really is—your life span—you will always ask the wrong question.

Until you embrace the whole of your Time and shape it accordingly, you will never be able to fully appreciate the moment.

Until you fully appreciate every second that comprises Time, you will never be sufficiently motivated to live those seconds fully.

Until you're sufficiently motivated to live those seconds fully, you will never see fit to change the way you are. You will never take the quality and sanctity of Time seriously.

And unless you take the sanctity of Time seriously, you will continue to struggle to catch up with something behind you. Your frustrations will mount as you try to snatch the second that just whisked by.

If you constantly fret about time with a small "t," then big-"T" Time will blow right past you. And you'll miss the whole point, the real truth about Time: You can't manage it; you never could. You can only *live* it.

And so that leaves you with these questions: How do I live my life? How do I give significance to it? How can I be here now, in this moment?

Once you begin to ask these questions, you'll find yourself moving toward a much fuller, richer life. But if you continue to be caught up in the banal work you do every day, you're never going to find the time to take a deep breath, exhale, and be present in the now.

So let's see what Riley has to say about time, and then we will talk about the subject of *work*. ✤

CHAPTER 22

What Time
Do You Have?

Riley F. Uglum

As if you could kill time without injuring eternity.

—Henry David Thoreau

Heavy stuff reading about Michael's description of time, isn't it? Not as heavy as Stephen Hawking, mind you, but heavy enough just the same. There are so many ways to think about time, organize time, schedule time, prioritize time, and feel about time. How do we feel about time? When all is said and done, is this the real question?

Michael talks about the optometrist who "downloaded" much of his nondoctor responsibilities to staff, which frees up doctor time. As described earlier in the book, I have been doing this for some time. And I continue to find ways to free up even more time in the optometry practice. How does this feel? It feels good. I can't imagine feeling like I did before I learned to clone myself and leverage staff and technology to do all but the activities requiring doctor input.

When Time Feels Right

The next question is, "How do we use the time that we free up?" And maybe an even more important question is, "How do we feel about our utilization of this time?"

We could use our freed-up time by goofing off. After all, working both harder and smarter than the average OD should entitle us to reap some well-deserved rewards, right? But in my case, the goof-off time didn't feel right after the first few months. Yet there were certain times when time did feel right. And as often as not, these times happened when I was seeing patients instead of goofing off during my well-earned goof-off time. So what was happening here? Shouldn't the quality time be happening when I'm not working? You would think so, but yet there were these isolated islands of time when I was totally engaged with a patient, and they definitely felt right!

When I enrolled in E-Myth Mastery and started learning how to strategically think about my business, there were more of these feel-right moments. But for the most part, I was feeling like the time I spent in the past could have been used more wisely, or that I needed to plan my future time carefully so that it would not be misspent. I was never in the *now*.

What I'm trying to say here boils down to this: Being in the now is precisely where time feels right!

In the Zone—in the Now

Easier said than done, however. Athletes call it "being in the zone." But even they can't be there all of the time. However, they have trained themselves to get there much more often than the average athlete. I get it on the golf course once in a while, and it is absolutely wonderful. I picture the shot and just let my body do what it needs for proper execution. There are no swing thoughts, no thoughts about previous shots, and no thoughts about what might happen after this shot. It's just the here and now and being totally in the moment. And then I stand in amazement watching the ball do exactly as I imagined it would. Time feels great!

Can I do this all the time? No. But I'm learning how to do it more often simply because it feels so wonderful. I know that my life is more meaningful (to me and to those I care about) when I feel and use my time in this manner. Yes, it's Zen-type stuff, and I used to think it was total nonsense. Not anymore.

The previous example occurs in a nonbusiness setting. But time can also feel great in a clinical setting when I devote my full attention to the concerns of the patient I'm engaged with. There are no thoughts of what happened with previous patients or what will happen afterward. I'm able to do this because I know I have a competent team running efficient systems that ensure everything else happens without me. Therefore, the patient gets my full attention and time feels great for both of us. Of course, this enables a patient experience that truly creates outstanding value and sets our business apart.

Change Your Business, Change Your Time

So for me, the quality of my life is being defined by how many of these "time feels great" moments I can create for myself and others between now and the day I die. And the really cool discovery here is that we can design our business to provide these moments for us. Indeed, the business development process itself can be a great source for these moments. This is especially true if our business supports our primary aim in life.

Before E-Myth, I don't remember having many of these time-feels-good moments. I was too busy "doing it." So what was it about E-Myth that allowed me to start living in the now? How did I break out of the time trap and start to live my life in a more meaningful manner? The answer to these questions was discovering my primary aim and designing my business and life to support it. Understanding this concept allows you to:

- Do what you love to do.
- Do what you are good at.
- Delegate what you aren't good at to those who are.
- Build a team whose abilities complement each other.
- Build a business that enhances the lives of everyone associated with it.

Most optometrists believe that vacations and retirement are what quality time is all about. They constantly look to the future for meaningful time (or to the past, wishing they had made it more meaningful). And that means they never live in, nor enjoy the moment at hand. So they also never learn how to truly enjoy their vacations or retirement for the same reason.

Retirement has become a foreign concept to me. At Promethean Ventures, we often ask clients this question: "If you were doing what you truly love to do, why would you ever want to stop doing it?" One definition of retire is "to take out of service." Is this a worthy goal in life? Do you want to exchange your "doing it, doing it, doing it" time for "taken out of service" time and call that your life? Is this what your Time—your life—is all about?

I believe a better solution is to learn the all-important time management skill of living your life "in the now." And it starts with learning how to do the proper type of work, which will be discussed in the next chapter.

Quantity versus Quality of Time

This chapter deals with how to make the most of the time we are given on this planet, i.e. *quality* of time. But it is also interesting to note that science now tells us that we can affect the *quantity* of the time we have here. I mention this because my businesses are actively engaged in using these new concepts to extend the quality and quantity of the lives of our patients and clients. Here are some things we already know:

- Life expectancy has increased in the United States (63.6 years in 1940 versus 77.9 years in 2009).
- The number of centenarians is increasing (38,300 in 1990 versus 104,099 in 2010).

When I started practicing in the mid-'70s, it was a rare thing to see a ninety-year-old patient. Now we see one or two every day. One day not too long ago we had six ninety-plus-year-olds on the same day. And many of them are still living independently in their homes. Why is this happening?

Americans are becoming more health-conscious. They are more active physically and mentally. They are starting to understand the importance of nutrition, so their diets are improving. And of course, there have been significant advances in health care over the past thirty years.

So could we as optometrists help our patients improve not only their longevity but their quality of life? Actually, we can do exactly that. New technologies allow us to measure critical biomarkers for aging, which can then be improved by employing a variety of new therapies. Our patients love the fact that we can now help them reduce the risk of aging changes. They can then increase the quality and quantity of their time. And of course, this sets our business apart from those that still use the traditional strategy of treating eyes after they become diseased. ❧

CHAPTER 23

On the Subject of Work

Michael E. Gerber

*As we learn we always change, and so our perception. This changed
perception then becomes a new Teacher inside each of us.*

　　　　　　　　　　　　　　　　　　—Hyemeyohsts Storm

In the business world, as the saying goes, the entrepreneur knows
something about everything, the technician knows everything
about something, and the switchboard operator just knows everything.

In an optometry practice, optometrists see their natural work as
the work of the technician. The Supreme Technician. Often to the
exclusion of everything else.

After all, optometrists get zero preparation working as a manager
and spend no time thinking as an entrepreneur—those just aren't
courses offered in today's schools and colleges of optometry. By the
time they own their own optometry practice, they're just doing it,
doing it, doing it.

At the same time, they want everything—freedom, respect,
money. Most of all, they want to rid themselves of meddling bosses

and start their own practice. That way they can be their own boss and take home all the money. These optometrists are in the throes of an entrepreneurial seizure.

Optometrists who have been praised for their amazing clinical skills believe they have what it takes to run an optometry practice. It's not unlike the plumber who becomes a contractor because he's a great plumber. Sure, he may be a great plumber . . . but it doesn't necessarily follow that he knows how to build a practice that does this work.

It's the same for an optometrist. So many of them are surprised to wake up one morning and discover that they're nowhere near as equipped for owning their own practice as they thought they were.

More than any other subject, work is the cause of obsessive-compulsive behavior by optometrists.

Work. You've got to do it every single day.

Work. If you fall behind, you'll pay for it.

Work. There's either too much or not enough.

So many optometrists describe work as what they do when they're busy. Some discriminate between the work they *could* be doing as optometrists and the work they *should* be doing as optometrists.

But according to the E-Myth, they're exactly the same thing. The work you *could* do and the work you *should* do as an optometrist are identical. Let me explain.

Strategic Work versus Tactical Work

Optometrists can do only two kinds of work: strategic work and tactical work.

Tactical work is easier to understand, because it's what almost every optometrist does almost every minute of every hour of every day. It's called getting the job done. It's called doing business.

Tactical work includes pretesting, refracting, special testing, patient education, managing staff, marketing, filing, billing, bookkeeping, dictating letters, charting, returning calls, going to the bank, and seeing patients.

The E-Myth says that tactical work is all the work optometrists find themselves doing in an optometry practice to *avoid* doing the strategic work.

"I'm too busy," most optometrists will tell you.

"How come nothing goes right unless I do it myself?" they complain in frustration.

Optometrists say these things when they're up to their ears in tactical work. But most optometrists don't understand that if they had done more strategic work, they would have less tactical work to do.

Optometrists are doing strategic work when they ask the following questions:

- Why am I an optometrist?
- What will my practice look like when it's done?
- What must my practice look, act, and feel like in order for it to compete successfully?
- What are the key indicators of my practice?

Please note that I said optometrists *ask* these questions when they are doing strategic work. I didn't say these are the questions they necessarily answer.

That is the fundamental difference between strategic work and tactical work. Tactical work is all about *answers*: How to do this. How to do that.

Strategic work, in contrast, is all about *questions*: What practice are we really in? Why are we in that practice? Who specifically is our practice determined to serve? When will I sell this practice? How and where will this practice be doing business when I sell it? And so forth.

Not that strategic questions don't have answers. Optometrists who commonly ask strategic questions know that once they ask such a question, they're already on their way to *envisioning* the answer. Question and answer are part of a whole. You can't find the right answer until you've asked the right question.

Tactical work is much easier, because the question is always more obvious. In fact, you don't ask the tactical question; instead, the question arises from a result you need to get or from a problem you need to solve. Billing a patient is tactical work. Fitting a patient for contact lenses is tactical work. Firing an employee is tactical work. Diagnosing glaucoma is tactical work.

Tactical work is the stuff you do every day in your practice. Strategic work is the stuff you plan to do to create an exceptional practice/business/enterprise.

In tactical work, the question comes from *out there* rather than *in here*. The tactical question is about something *outside* of you, whereas the strategic question is about something *inside* of you.

The tactical question is about something you *need* to do, whereas the strategic question is about something you *want* to do. Want versus need.

If tactical work consumes you:

- You are always reacting to something outside of you.
- Your practice runs you; you don't run it.
- Your employees run you; you don't run them.
- Your life runs you; you don't run your life.

You must understand that the more strategic work you do, the more intentional your decisions, your practice, and your life become. *Intention* is the byword of strategic work.

Everything on the outside begins to serve you, to serve your vision, rather than forcing you to serve it. Everything you *need* to do is congruent with what you *want* to do. It means you have a vision, an aim, a purpose, a strategy, an *envisioned* result.

Strategic work is the work you do to *design* your practice, to design your life.

Tactical work is the work you do to *implement* the design created by strategic work.

Without strategic work, there is no design. Without strategic work, all that's left is keeping busy.

There's only one thing left to do. It's time to take *action*. And we'll do that right after Riley gives us his views on work. ❧

CHAPTER 24

The Reason Behind the Work

Riley F. Uglum

We cannot solve our problems with the same level of thinking that created them.

—Albert Einstein

I recently visited with the head of cardiothoracic surgery at a prestigious hospital (he had just performed surgery on my son). He had the whole package: impressive certificates on the wall, celebrity clients, large paychecks, and plus, he was just a nice guy. Easy to talk to and no ego to deal with. It struck me that this is what many doctors aspire to. It also occurred to me that this surgeon still had a job—a great job—but a job for which he exchanges his time for money. He was a technician doing tactical work (at a very high level of expertise). Imagine if he were to become disenchanted with this arrangement and strike out on his own to become an entrepreneurial doctor.

Let's say, for instance, that the surgeon gets tired of conforming to hospital policies and would like to have better control of his work schedule. He also knows he can generate more income by going into business for himself. So he opens his own practice to escape from his "job." But what he quickly realizes is that despite the improved revenue, he now needs to deal with:

- Marketing problems
- Accounts receivable problems
- Accounting problems
- Staff HR problems and benefit packages
- Unpaid vacations
- Doing it, doing it, doing it
- Tactical work

So much for having control of his time. Instead of becoming entrepreneurial, he simply exchanged one job for another. Despite his good intentions, he has further immersed himself into the tactical world. There is no time for strategic work. Does this sound familiar?

True Strategic Work

By contrast, I sat next to a man at a wedding reception last year whom I knew to be an expert in hearing aid technology. He has helped celebrities and presidents with their hearing problems for the past forty years. And he has scaled his business into many locations worldwide. He takes monthlong philanthropic trips to Third World countries to help those who desperately need his company's services, while his enterprise keeps right on running without him. I asked him if he had any technological or engineering background that allowed him to create and produce the amazing hearing aids his company provides. He replied, "Not really, but I employ a lot of PhDs that do."

Can you see the differences? The hearing aid entrepreneur had a vision of his business becoming the best hearing aid company in the world (strategic work) but he never became the chief technician in his business. He used money, planning, management, people, patients, growth, change, time, and work properly. He became truly free to pursue his primary aim in life and make the planet a better place on which to live.

Learning How to Do Strategic Work

So that, in a nutshell, that is what this book is really about. At Promethean Ventures, we call our process A Freedom Formula for Private Practice Optometrists. It's all about thinking differently about a doctor's work. Doctors certainly understand how to *work in* their practice and are usually doing this quite well. But to achieve true freedom in their lives, they need to understand how to *work on* their practice. They need to learn CEO skills.

But crossing the chasm from a technician's left-brain perspective to the CEO's right-brain, strategic world is difficult for optometrists. Think about it. From the time we first started thinking about an optometry career, we entered a left-brain technician's world. It was all about:

- Following a pre-optometry science curriculum and getting good grades
- Studying for and passing OCATs for entry into optometry school
- Following the optometry school curriculum and getting good grades
- Learning good clinical examination techniques
- Studying for and passing national boards
- Transferring our clinical skills to the real world
- Tactical/technical/nonstrategic work—doing it, doing it, doing it

There was strategic work going on here (not ours), and it was all about creating good optometric physicians. We, as optometry students, simply followed someone else's strategic process from a technician's perspective. We never learned how to develop our own strategic skills.

So how do we make that transition now that we are full-fledged left-brain optometrists? Well, as Michael would say, it all starts with asking strategic questions like: "What would my practice look like if it were able to reflect my dreams, values, and purpose in life?"

Hmm—I don't seem to remember any courses in optometry school called Creating Your Vision 101, or Living Your Dream 201. No, it was all left-brain, tactical stuff. But unless you do the strategic work of creating your vision, you will never be free from tactically "doing it" for the rest of your life.

Questions Are the Key

Asking strategic questions causes us to more closely examine our dreams, values, and "soul purpose." And this examination is most often uncomfortable for us because as optometrists, we are such left-brained, technical animals. We simply can't comprehend dreaming about something without having all of the dots connected in advance. It is a dramatic leap of faith for a technician to imagine his or her practice at a much higher level and not see each step along the way. But competent CEOs always have a bold vision. They trust that they will find the right people, tools, and strategies along the way that will help them get there (otherwise known as building the airplane as you fly it).

You may recall that in Chapter 14 on estimating, asking the proper question was the key to solving a seemingly unsolvable problem. The very act of asking these questions is strategic work. And there you have it! This is the first step in bridging the gap from a technical to a strategic mindset. It doesn't really seem like work because you were just thinking. You didn't bill a procedure or create any direct revenue. You weren't busy doing something or reacting to something. You didn't exchange your time for money!

But as we learned about time, you have only so much of it. If you try to exchange it all for money, there won't be very many moments of quality time left to enjoy. And there will be a limited amount of money that you can make due to the limited amount of time that you have. The alternative is using your time to live your primary aim through your business. That's true freedom.

Imagine doing what you love to do every day and getting paid for it. Imagine having a business that serves you. How would you do that? If you don't take the time to do the right kind of work, ask the right questions, and envision the result you want, you will never get there.

Transitioning Tactical to Strategic

I remember years ago watching the end of a golf tournament in which the prize money was $250,000 (a lot more money at that time than it is now). Greg Norman won the tournament, and in his post-tournament interview he was asked to comment on how it feels win that much money. His answer amazed me at the time. He said something to the effect that a quarter million dollars was nice but that he was concentrating more on cultivating his business skills, and that he admired his friends who were very business-savvy and made a lot more money than he did. I didn't get it at the time, but Greg knew he was exchanging his time for money on the golf course and couldn't do it forever.

We can see today that because of his clothing line, the Norman wine label, the real estate deals, and his golf course design business, Greg's financial affairs are in great shape and he can play golf for fun. He simply leveraged his tactical golf work into entrepreneurial strategic work and is now having the time of his life. How about you? How would you like to do optometry for fun while living your life in an environment of entrepreneurial freedom? ❧

CHAPTER 25

On the Subject of Taking Action

Michael E. Gerber

Deliberation is the work of many men. Action, of one alone.
—Charles de Gaulle

It's time to get started, time to take action. Time to stop thinking about the old practice and start thinking about the new practice. It's not a matter of coming up with better practices; it's about reinventing the practice of optometry.

And the optometrist has to take personal responsibility for it.

That's you.

So sit up and pay attention!

You, the optometrist, have to be interested. You cannot abdicate accountability for the practice of optometry, the administration of optometry, or the finance of optometry.

Although the goal is to create systems into which optometrists can plug reasonably competent people—systems that allow the practice to run without them—optometrists must take responsibility for that happening.

I can hear the chorus now: "But we're optometrists! We shouldn't have to know about this." To that I say: whatever. If you don't give a flip about your practice, fine—close your mind to new knowledge and accountability. But if you want to succeed, then you better step up and take responsibility, and you better do it now.

All too often, optometrists take no responsibility for the business of optometry but instead delegate tasks without any understanding of what it takes to do them; without any interest in what their people are actually doing; without any sense of what it feels like to be at the front desk when a patient comes in and has to wait for forty-five minutes; and without any appreciation for the entity that is creating their livelihood.

Optometrists can open the portals of change in an instant. All you have to do is say, "I don't want to do it that way anymore." Saying it will begin to set you free—even though you don't yet understand what the practice will look like after it's been reinvented.

This demands an intentional leap from the known into the unknown. It further demands that you live there—in the unknown—for a while. It means discarding the past, everything you once believed to be true.

Think of it as soaring rather than plunging.

Thought Control

You should now be clear about the need to organize your thoughts first, then your business. Because the organization of your thoughts is the foundation for the organization of your business.

If we try to organize our business without organizing our thoughts, we will fail to attack the problem.

We have seen that organization is not simply time management. Nor is it people management. Nor is it tidying up desks or alphabetizing patient files. Organization is first, last, and always cleaning up the mess of our minds.

By learning how to *think* about the practice of optometry, by learning how to *think* about your priorities, and by learning how to *think* about your life, you'll prepare yourself to do righteous battle with the forces of failure.

Right thinking leads to right action—and now is the time to take action. Because it is only through action that you can translate thoughts into movement in the real world, and, in the process, find fulfillment.

So, first, *think* about what you want to do. Then *do* it. Only in this way will you be fulfilled.

How do you put the principles we've discussed in this book to work in your optometry practice?

To find out, accompany me down the path once more:

Create a story about your practice. Your story should be an idealized version of your optometry practice, a vision of what the pre-eminent optometrist in your field should be and why. Your story must become the very heart of your practice. It must become the spirit that mobilizes it, as well as everyone who walks through the doors. Without this story, your practice will be reduced to plain work.

Organize your practice so that it breathes life into your story. Unless your practice can faithfully replicate your story in action, it all becomes fiction. In that case, you'd be better off not telling your story at all. And without a story, you'd be better off leaving your practice the way it is and just hoping for the best.

Here are some tips for organizing your optometry practice:

- Identify the key functions of your practice.
- Identify the essential processes that link those functions.
- Identify the results you have determined your practice will produce.
- Clearly state in writing how each phase will work.

Take it step by step. Think of your practice as a program, a piece of software, a system. It is a collaboration, a collection of processes dynamically interacting with one another.

Of course, your practice is also people.

Engage your people in the process. Why is this the third step rather than the first? Because, contrary to the advice most business experts will give you, you must never engage your people in the process until you yourself are clear about what you intend to do.

The need for consensus is a disease of today's addled mind. It's a product of our troubled and confused times. When people don't know what to believe in, they often ask others to tell them. To ask is not to lead but to follow.

The prerequisite of sound leadership is first to know where you wish to go.

And so, "What do *I* want?" becomes the first question; not, "What do *they* want?" In your own practice, the vision must first be yours. To follow another's vision is to abdicate your personal accountability, your leadership role, your true power.

In short, the role of leader cannot be delegated or shared. And without leadership, no optometry practice will ever succeed.

Despite what you have been told, *win-win* is a secondary step, not a primary one. The opposite of *win-win* is not necessarily *they lose*.

Let's say "they" can win by choosing a good horse. The best choice will not be made by consensus. "Guys, what horse do you think we should ride?" will always lead to endless and worthless discussions. By the time you're done jawing, the horse will have already left the post.

Before you talk to your people about what you intend to do in your practice and why you intend to do it, you need to reach agreement with yourself.

It's important to know (1) *exactly* what you want, (2) how you intend to proceed, (3) what's important to you and what isn't, and (4) what you want the practice to be and how you want it to get there.

Once you have that agreement, it's critical that you engage your people in a discussion about what you intend to do and why. Be clear—both with yourself and with them.

The Story

The story is paramount because it is your vision. Tell it with passion and conviction. Tell it with precision. Never hurry a great story. Unveil it slowly. Don't mumble or show embarrassment. Never apologize or display false modesty. Look your audience in the eyes and tell your story as though it is the most important one they'll ever hear about business. Your business. The business into which you intend to pour your heart, your soul, your intelligence, your imagination, your time, your money, and your sweaty persistence.

Get into the storytelling zone. Behave as though it means everything to you. Show no equivocation when telling your story.

These tips are important because you're going to tell your story over and over—to patients, to new and old employees, to optometrists, to associate optometrists, to opticians, and to your family and friends. You're going to tell it at your church or synagogue; to your card-playing or fishing buddies; and to organizations such as Kiwanis, Rotary, YMCA, Hadassah, and Boy Scouts.

There are few moments in your life when telling a great story about a great business is inappropriate.

If it is to be persuasive, you must love your story. Do you think Walt Disney loved his Disneyland story? Or Ray Kroc his McDonald's story? What about Dave Smith at Federal Express? Or Debbie Fields at Mrs. Fields Cookies? Or Tom Watson Jr. at IBM?

Do you think these people loved their stories? Do you think others loved (and *still* love) to hear them? I daresay *all* successful entrepreneurs have loved the story of their business. Because that's what true entrepreneurs do. They tell stories that come to life in the form of their business.

Remember: A great story never fails. A great story is always a joy to hear.

In summary, you first need to clarify, both for yourself and for your people, the *story* of your practice. Then you need to detail the *process* your practice must go through to make your story become reality.

I call this the business development process. Others call it reengineering, continuous improvement, reinventing your practice, or total quality management.

Whatever you call it, you must take three distinct steps to succeed:

1. *Innovation.* Continue to find better ways of doing what you do.

2. *Quantification.* Once that is achieved, quantify the impact of these improvements on your practice.

3. *Orchestration.* Once these improvements are verified, orchestrate this better way of running your practice so that it becomes your standard, to be repeated time and again.

In this way, the system works—no matter who's using it. And you've built a practice that works consistently, predictably, systematically. A practice you can depend on to operate exactly as promised, every single time.

Your vision, your people, your process—all linked.

A superior optometry practice is a creation of your imagination, a product of your mind. So fire it up and get started like Riley did. He'll tell you about it in the next chapter. ❖

26

Taking Action

Riley F. Uglum

The way to get started is to quit talking and begin doing.

—Walt Disney

I once read a sign that said "Fail Faster." I didn't understand it initially, but I do now. In essence, it tells us that taking some kind of action is preferable to doing nothing. Because even if that action fails, we learn something from it that will make us better in the future. So the logic is that the faster we fail, the faster we learn, and that we can improve ourselves at an accelerated rate.

This philosophy has merit, although we need to be reasonably certain that the action is moving us toward our strategic objectives. And of course, our strategic objectives should reflect our primary aim. In other words, there needs to be some strategic thinking work done in advance which then helps us determine if a particular tactical action makes sense.

Before E-Myth, I subscribed to a looser version of Fail Faster. I often initiated change for the sake of change. So on a

173

whim, I might tinker with the appointment schedule to try and improve our efficiency. But I would totally fail to appreciate how difficult that might make life for the rest of my team, or how it could affect patient perceptions with longer wait times. So the indiscriminate action was tied to one practice metric: increased gross production. But it didn't respect any of our other strategic objectives—because there weren't any. This same scenario played itself out time after time. Sometimes the action would work out, but as often as not it didn't. Of course, I always learned from my mistakes, but it was E-Myth that showed me the error of my ways.

Action plus Thinking

My business is still very action-oriented, but all action is determined by the positive effect it will have on our strategic objectives. Systems are employed to ensure that this happens. And the systems need not be complex. One of the most simple but effective systems we have is called the twenty-four-hour rule. It simply states that we make no major business decision, regardless of how good it looks, till we think about it for twenty-four hours. Then, if no major downside is anticipated and the upside is still solid, we take action.

Another thing I can speak to regarding action is taking advantage of opportunities when they present themselves. This usually happens after we seriously do the strategic work and ask questions like, "What would my practice look like if …?

Questions Engage Your Right Brain

Michael and other successful entrepreneurs told me that opportunities would appear if I asked the right questions, but as a left-brained optometrist, I remained skeptical. So when it started happening, I sometimes didn't even realize it. Opportunities in disguise are what I call them now.

It's amazing how asking the right questions will elicit answers in strange ways. The key is recognizing them when they appear, performing due diligence (to ensure they support our strategic objectives), and then taking action if appropriate.

Football is all about action. But there are many strategic questions asked prior to a game. Offensive systems are innovated so as to capitalize on the opposition's weakness. Defensive systems are tweaked to take away the opponent's advantages. It is only after the strategic questions have been asked and answered that tactical action is executed.

Professional trading is also about action. In a previous life, I trained under two of the top technical trading coaches in the world, Van Tharp and Ken Long. Although I realized eventually that trading didn't fit my primary aim, I learned a lot about life and business from these guys. Technical trading can be a stressful way to make a living and definitely involves action. But I learned that successful traders rely on strategic systems that are then executed in a disciplined, tactical way while removing all emotion.

Meditation is a common practice among these types, which is not what you would expect when you look at the occupation superficially. But it helps them stay connected to their right brain strategically and tempers their emotions in the heat of battle so that their actions always reflect the strategic work they have done. I now consider meditation an indispensable CEO skill.

Tactical Systems Engage the Right Brain

Ken, who is a retired lieutenant colonel in the Army Rangers, has a master's degree in systems management and still teaches at the U.S. Army Command and General Staff College. The systems he manages are usually employed in combat situations. He once told me why the United States is superior militarily to every other nation in the world. It is because of its after-action reporting system. After every combat engagement or exercise, commanders look at what went right and wrong with the tactical systems they employed. If a particular tactical action produces an undesirable strategic result, certain questions are asked:

- Where did the tactical system break down?
- Why did it break down?
- What would this system look like to prevent future breakdowns?

The answers to these questions shed light on the action that produced the undesirable result so it can be innovated to better support the strategic objectives. Likewise, desirable results are analyzed so they can be faithfully reproduced. In essence, what we have here is a very refined "fail faster" system. And it works better than any other in the world.

Ken designs his trading systems the same way and with equally superior results. Trading and military combat are really just other forms of business when looked at from an E-Myth perspective. And we can see how effective action is when combined with superior strategic work.

The one caution here is the "paralysis by overanalysis" trap. Once the strategic work has been done and a course of action has been determined, *then make it so!*

I like to think of Captain Jean-Luc Picard (played by Patrick Stewart) in *Star Trek: The Next Generation* in these situations. Whenever he was confronted with difficult decisions, he would weigh his options, listen to suggestions from other members of his team, pick what he considered his best option, and then simply order his crew to "make it so." It was time for action.

Why not take the proper action with your practice and transform it into a business that supports your life's dreams? I sincerely hope that this book is a catalyst for action on your part in the same way that reading Michael's *The E-Myth Revisited* was for me. I'm here to help when you are ready. ❦

AFTERWORD

Michael E. Gerber

For more than three decades, I've applied the E-Myth principles I've shared with you in this book to the successful development of thousands of small businesses throughout the world. Many have been optometry practices—with optometrists specializing in everything from pediatric eye care to ocular disease to contact lenses.

Few rewards are greater than seeing these E-Myth principles improve the work and lives of so many people. Those rewards include seeing these changes:

- Lack of clarity—clarified
- Lack of organization—organized
- Lack of direction—shaped into a path that is clearly, lovingly, passionately pursued
- Lack of money or money poorly managed—money understood instead of coveted; created instead of chased; wisely spent or invested instead of squandered
- Lack of committed people—transformed into a cohesive community working in harmony toward a common goal; discovering each other and themselves in the process; all the while expanding their understanding, their know-how, their interest, their attention

After working with so many optometrists, I know that a practice can be much more than what most become. I also know that nothing is preventing you from making your practice all that it can be. It takes only desire and the perseverance to see it through.

In this book—the next in the E-Myth Expert series—the E-Myth principles have been complemented and enriched by stories from Dr. Riley F. Uglum, a real-life optometrist who has put these principles to use in his practice. Riley had the desire and perseverance to achieve success beyond his wildest dreams. Now you, too, can join his ranks.

I hope this book has helped you clear your vision and set your sights on a very bright future.

To your practice!

ABOUT THE AUTHORS

Michael E. Gerber

Michael E. Gerber is the legend behind the E-Myth series of books, which includes *The E-Myth Revisited, E-Myth Mastery, The E-Myth Manager, The E-Myth Enterprise* and *Awakening the Entrepreneur Within*. Collectively, his books have sold millions of copies worldwide. He is the founder of In the Dreaming Room™, a 2½-day process to awaken the entrepreneur within, and Origination, which trains facilitators to assist entrepreneurs in growing "turnkey" businesses. He is chairman of the Michael E. Gerber Companies. A highly sought-after speaker and consultant, he has trained more than 70,000 businesses in his career. Michael lives with his wife Luz Delia, in Carlsbad, California.

ABOUT THE AUTHORS

Riley F. Uglum

R iley F. Uglum, OD, is the founder of three companies: Eye Care Associates of New Hampton, an innovative optometry practice that creates services and products to fulfill patients' needs; Promethean Ventures, a company that provides advanced business systems and wealth-building strategies for private practice optometrists; and The National Wellness Alliance, which helps entrepreneurial doctors expand their preventative health care services in the growing anti-aging market.

All these companies operate with E-Myth systems as their foundation. Without them, Dr. Uglum would still be living the "Entrepreneurial Myth" as an optometrist, instead of being free to pursue his dreams. He lives with his wife Kathy in New Hampton, Iowa.

ABOUT THE SERIES

The E-Myth expert series brings Michael E. Gerber's proven E-Myth philosophy to a wide variety of different professional practice areas. The E-Myth, short for "Entrepreneurial Myth," is simple: too many small businesses fail to grow because their leaders think like technicians, not entrepreneurs. Gerber's approach gives small enterprise leaders practical, proven methods that have already helped transform more than 70,000 businesses. Let the E-Myth expert series boost your professional practice today!

Books in the series include:
The E-Myth Attorney
The E-Myth Accountant
The E-Myth Optometrist
The E-Myth Chiropractor
The E-Myth Financial Advisor

Forthcoming books in the series include:
The E-Myth Landscape Contractor
The E-Myth Rainmaker
The E-Myth Real Estate Investor
The E-Myth Real Estate Brokerage
. . . and 300 more industries and professions

Learn more at: www.michaelegerber.com/co-author

Have you created an E-Myth enterprise? Would you like to become a co-author of an E-Myth book in your industry? Go to www.michaelegerber.com/co-author.

THE MICHAEL E. GERBER
ENTREPRENEUR'S LIBRARY
It Keeps Growing...

Thank you for reading another E-Myth Vertical book.

Who do you know who is an expert in their industry?

Who has applied The E-Myth to the improvement of their
practice as Riley F. Uglum, OD has?

Who can add immense value to others in his or her industry
by sharing what he or she has learned?

Please share this book with that individual and share that individual with us.

We at Michael E. Gerber Companies are determined to transform the state
of small business and entrepreneurship worldwide. *You can help.*

To find out more, email us at Michael E. Gerber Partners, at
gerber@michaelegerber.com.

To find out how YOU can apply the E-Myth to YOUR practice,
contact us at gerber@michaelegerber.com.

Thank you for living your Dream, and changing the world.

Authors of Business Design

Michael E. Gerber, Co-Founder/Chairman
Michael E. Gerber Companies™
Creator of The E-Myth Evolution™
P.O. Box 131195, Carlsbad, CA 92013
760-752-1812 O • 760-752-9926 F
gerber@michaelegerber.com
www.michaelegerber.com

Join The Evolution^{SM}

Find the latest updates:
www.michaelegerber.com

Attend the Dreaming Room Trainings
www.michaelegerber.com

Listen to the Michael E. Gerber Radio Show
www.blogtalkradio.com/michaelegerber

Watch the latest videos
www.youtube.com/michaelegerber

Connect on LinkedIn
www.linkedin.com/in/michaelegerber

Connect on Facebook
www.facebook.com/MichaelEGerberCo

Follow on Twitter
http://twitter.com/michaelegerber

CPSIA information can be obtained
at www.ICGtesting.com
Printed in the USA
LVHW031922230222
711809LV00013B/473/J